25 Years of
India-ASEAN Economic Co-operation

25 Years of India-ASEAN Economic Co-operation

By

Vishal Sarin
Associate Professor and Head (Economics),
Mittal School of Business,
Lovely Professional University (LPU),
Phagwara, Punjab

New Century Publications
New Delhi, India

NEW CENTURY PUBLICATIONS
4800 / 24, Bharat Ram Road,
Ansari Road, Daryaganj,
New Delhi - 110 002 (India)

Tel.: 011-2324 7798, 4358 7398, 4101 7798
E-mail: indiatax@vsnl.com • info@newcenturypublications.com
www.newcenturypublications.com

Editorial office:
LG – 7, Aakarshan Bhawan,
4754-57/23, Ansari Road, Daryaganj,
New Delhi – 110 002

Tel.: 011-4356 0919

First Published: **2019**

ISBN: **978-81-7708-475-7**

Published by New Century Publications and printed at Milan Enterprises, New Delhi.

Designs: Patch Creative Unit, New Delhi.

PRINTED IN INDIA

About the Book

India has always stood for an open, equitable, predictable, non-discriminatory and rule-based international trading system. It views regional trade agreements (RTAs) as building blocks in the overall objective of trade liberalization as well as complementing the multilateral trading system under the World Trade Organization (WTO). India has been actively engaging in regional and bilateral trade negotiations with a view to diversify and expand the markets for its exports as well as ensuring access to raw materials, intermediates and capital goods for stimulating value added domestic manufacturing.

India unveiled its *Look East* policy in 1991. East Asia (including Japan, China, South Korea and ASEAN) is today India's largest trading partner. India's engagement with the Association of Southeast Asian Nations (ASEAN) started with its *Look East* policy. ASEAN has a membership of 10 countries, namely Brunei Darussalam, Cambodia, Indonesia, Lao PDR, Malaysia, Myanmar, Philippines, Singapore, Thailand and Vietnam. India became a Sectoral Dialogue Partner of ASEAN in 1992 and Full Dialogue Partner in 1996. In November 2001, the ASEAN-India relationship was upgraded to the summit level.

Heads of State/Government of the Member States of ASEAN and the Republic of India gathered in New Delhi on January 25, 2018 to commemorate the 25th Anniversary of ASEAN-India Dialogue Relations under the theme of 'Shared Values, Common Destiny'. They reaffirmed their commitment to guide ASEAN-India Dialogue Relations by the principles, shared values and norms enshrined in the Charter of the United Nations.

This book traces the course of India-ASEAN economic relations, focusing on trade. It provides an in-depth analysis of trade flows between India and the ASEAN countries in recent years.

About the Author

Dr. Vishal Sarin is presently Associate Professor and Head (Economics), Mittal School of Business, Lovely Professional University (LPU), Phagwara, Punjab. He obtained his Ph.D. degree from Punjabi University, Patiala in 2014. He has published a number of research papers in reputed journals including *International Journal of Agricultural and Statistical Science, International Journal of Economic Research, International Journal of Multi-disciplinary Research* and *Research Journal in Social Sciences*. He has attended and presented papers at various national level conferences/seminars.

Dr. Vishal is the author of the book titled *India-ASEAN Trade and Economic Relations.* He is a life member of Indian Economic Association and a member of the editorial advisory board of *ENVISION: International Journal of Commerce and Management*.

Contents

Preface

Regional trade agreements (RTAs) are efforts by nations aimed at deepening economic relations, usually with neighbouring countries, and tend to be largely political in nature. With the multilateral trade negotiations process under the WTO being a painfully slow one requiring broad-based consensus, RTAs have progressively assumed greater importance and a growing share in international trade. While RTAs are broadly compliant with WTO mandates, they remain second-best solutions that are discriminatory in nature against non-members and are inefficient as low cost producing non-members lose out to members.

India has always stood for an open, equitable, predictable, non-discriminatory and rule-based international trading system and views RTAs as building blocks in the overall objective of trade liberalization as well as complementing the multilateral trading system under the WTO. India has been actively engaging in regional and bilateral trade negotiations with a view to diversifying and expanding the markets for its exports as well as ensuring access to raw materials, intermediates and capital goods for stimulating value added domestic manufacturing.

RTAs are an integral part of India's foreign trade policy, complementing the multilateral trading system. Prior to economic reforms process initiated in 1991, India had adopted a very cautious and guarded approach to regionalism. Recognising that RTAs would continue to feature prominently in world trade, India engaged with its trading partners/blocks with the intention of expanding its export market and began concluding in principle agreements and moving in some cases even towards Comprehensive Economic Cooperation Agreements (CECAs) which cover Free Trade Agreements (FTAs) in goods, services, investments and identified areas of economic cooperation.

India unveiled the *Look East* policy in 1991. East Asia (including Japan, China, South Korea and ASEAN) is today India's largest trading partner, ahead of EU and the US.

Proliferation of Free Trade Agreements (FTAs) is the clearest evidence of Asian countries' desire to forge closer economic relationships. The growing importance of CECA's indicates that such agreements are becoming deeper, extending to areas beyond just tariff reduction. Intra-regional trade and investment require building up of shared infrastructure. Many Asian countries have joined together to develop cross-border infrastructure to lay the foundations for closer trading relationships and increased connectivity among countries.

Asia remains one of the least integrated regions lacking a continent-wide regional organization. Forging closer links among Asian nations through appropriate institutional mechanisms can lead to substantial enhancement of national, regional and global productivity and output. In the past, India had adopted a very cautious approach to regionalism, and was engaged in only a few bilateral/regional initiatives, mainly through Preferential Trade Agreements (PTAs).

India's engagement with the Association of South East Asian Nations (ASEAN) started with its *Look East* policy in the year 1991. ASEAN has a membership of 10 countries, namely Brunei Darussalam, Cambodia, Indonesia, Lao PDR, Malaysia, Myanmar, Philippines, Singapore, Thailand and Vietnam. India became a Sectoral Dialogue Partner of ASEAN in 1992 and Full Dialogue Partner in 1996. In November 2001, the ASEAN-India relationship was upgraded to the summit level.

The First ASEAN Economic Ministers (AEM)-India Consultations were held on September 15, 2002 in Brunei Darussalam where the Ministers, after discussing the Joint Study Report decided to establish an ASEAN-India Economic Linkages Task Force (AIELTF). The AIELTF was asked to prepare a draft Framework Agreement to enhance the ASEAN-India trade and economic cooperation before the 2nd AEM-India Consultations. Subsequently, at the First ASEAN-India Summit held on November 5, 2002 in Phnom Penh, Cambodia, the Prime Minister of India made the following major announcements:

- India will extend special and differential trade treatment to

ASEAN countries, based on their levels of development to improve their market access to India; and

- FTA within 10 years timeframe.

A Framework Agreement on Comprehensive Economic Cooperation between the Association of Southeast Asian Nations (ASEAN) and India was signed by the Prime Minster of India and the Heads of Nation/Governments of ASEAN members during the Second ASEAN-India Summit on October 8, 2003 in Bali, Indonesia.

The key elements of the Framework Agreement on Comprehensive Economic Cooperation between ASEAN and India cover FTA in goods, services and investment, as well as Areas of Economic Cooperation. The Agreement also provided for an Early Harvest Programme (EHP) which covers areas of Economic Cooperation and a common list of items for exchange of tariff concessions as a confidence building measure.

Presently, the ASEAN-India Trade Negotiating Committee (TNC) is undertaking negotiations for a Comprehensive Economic Cooperation Agreement (CECA) which includes a Free Trade Area in goods, services and investment. Agreement has been reached on the Rules of Origin and Dispute Settlement Mechanism. The TNC is now negotiating the modalities for tariff reduction and elimination.

On August 13, 2009, India and ASEAN signed the Trade in Goods Agreement under the broader framework of a Comprehensive Economic Cooperation Agreement (CECA) between India and ASEAN. The Trade in Goods Agreement provides for elimination of basic customs duty on 80 percent of the tariff lines accounting for 75 percent of the trade in a gradual manner starting from January 1, 2010. India has excluded 489 HS 6 digit lines from the list of tariff concessions and 590 HS 6 digit lines from the list of tariff eliminations to address sensitivities in agriculture, textiles, auto, chemicals, crude and refined palm oil, coffee, tea, pepper etc.

India's focus on a strengthened and multi-faceted relationship with ASEAN is an outcome of the significant changes in the world's political and economic scenario since the early 1990s and India's own march towards economic liberalisation. India's search for economic space resulted in the 'Look East Policy'. The *Look East* policy has today matured into a dynamic and action oriented 'Act East Policy'.

India's relationship with ASEAN is a key pillar of foreign policy and the foundation of our Act East Policy. The up-gradation of the relationship into a Strategic Partnership in 2012 was a natural progression to the ground covered since India became a Sectoral Partner of the ASEAN in 1992, Dialogue Partner in 1996 and Summit Level Partner in 2002. There are, in total, 30 Dialogue Mechanisms between India and ASEAN, cutting across various sectors. India has set up a separate Mission to ASEAN and the EAS in Jakarta in April 2015 with a dedicated Ambassador to strengthen engagement with ASEAN and ASEAN-centric processes.

Heads of State/Government of the Member States of the Association of Southeast Asian Nations (ASEAN) and the Republic of India, gathered in New Delhi on January 25, 2018 to commemorate the 25th Anniversary of ASEAN-India Dialogue Relations under the theme of 'Shared Values, Common Destiny'. They reaffirmed their commitment to guide ASEAN-India Dialogue Relations by the principles, purposes, shared values and norms enshrined in the Charter of the United Nations, the Treaty of Amity and Cooperation in Southeast Asia (TAC), the Declaration of the East Asia Summit on the Principles for Mutually Beneficial Relations, and the Vision Statement adopted at the ASEAN-India Commemorative Summit to mark the 20th Anniversary of ASEAN-India Dialogue Relations on December 20, 2012 and supporting the ASEAN Charter.

Vishal Sarin

Abbreviations/Acronyms

AIFTA	ASEAN-India Free Trade Agreement
ASEAN	Association of Southeast Asian Nations
CP	Competitively Positioned
EP	Emerging Products
ET	Emerging Threatened Products
FDI	Foreign Direct Investment
FII	Foreign Institutional Investment
GDP	Gross Domestic Product
LFI	Lafay Index
LT	Less Threatened Products
RCA	Revealed Comparative Advantage
RD	Rising Dependence
RI	Rising Independence
RID	Revealed Import Dependency
SAARC	South Asian Association for Regional Cooperation
TP	Threatened Products
UNCOMTRADE	United Nations Commodity Trade
UNCTAD	United Nations Conference on Trade and Development
WP	Weakly Positioned
WTO	World Trade Organization

1

Globalization and World Trade

Fundamental changes have taken place in the pattern of international trade after the Second World War. These are detailed below.

1.1 Developments in International Trade: 1950 to 1980

The period 1950-1980 witnessed a revival of world trade, especially among the industrialised countries. This was facilitated by the economic reconstruction following the two World Wars and reduction in transportation costs. Another important factor contributing to trade expansion was the multilateral initiative under GATT that enabled dismantling of trade barriers and non-tariff barriers among the industrialised countries imposed during the inter-war period. The move towards currency convertibility on current account transactions by leading industrial powers which began in the late 1950s further facilitated growth in international trade.

Another phase of trade integration started during the late 1970s when a number of East Asian economies embarked on the path of export-led growth. This was reinforced further during the 1980s and the 1990s wherein a large number of developing countries gradually increased their degree of openness. During this period, outward-oriented policies were undertaken on the grounds of efficient resource allocation, infusion of modern technologies, promotion of economies of scale, retention of consumer surplus, and reduction of rent-seeking and unproductive profit-seeking activities. For Latin America, the necessity to regain access to the international capital markets to refinance outstanding debt was an important consideration in their opening up during the 1970s.

Contrary to the initiatives taken by the East Asian

economies during most of this phase, India could not take full advantage of greater openness in trade regime. Despite some export promotion measures undertaken in the 1970s, Indian industries continued to remain protected. While the signs of liberalised trade policy were clearly discernible in the latter half of 1980s, it was only in the 1990s that the country embarked on a truly liberalised trade regime.

Increasing trade openness by developed countries and later by developing economies resulted in significant changes in the pattern of world trade. The major structural changes witnessed can be summarised as follows.

1. Noticeable increase in Asia's share in world trade mainly due to high export growth of China and East Asia since 1980s.
2. Transformation of the export basket of developing countries from primary commodities to manufacturing exports.
3. Faster growth in exports of technology-intensive products by developing countries compared to industrialised economies.
4. Growth in the South-South trade.

In contrast to earlier periods, world economic integration in the 1990s was much more widespread and was primarily driven by liberalisation of trade and capital controls. The technological revolution witnessed in recent years and the emergence of the new economies further aided this integration process. As the process of opening up of economies unfolded during the 1990s, world trade witnessed its strongest revival in terms of volume growth. Although the real growth performance of Western Europe, Japan, the transitional economies of Central Europe and Africa was rather lacklustre during most of the 1990s, the strong revival in the volume of trade was mainly led by the US with support from developing countries including China, East Asia and some Latin American countries.

Although almost all of the East Asian countries posted double-digit trade growth during the 1990s up to 1997, trade expansion in these countries suffered a major setback following the crisis of 1997. Their performance took a severe downturn in the years immediately after the crisis. The impact of the East Asian crisis on growth in volume of exports was less pronounced than for imports.

China's trade performance (both exports and imports) continued to remain impressive throughout the 1990s. India too posted a healthy growth during the 1990s, especially during the initial years of economic reforms. Amongst the Latin American economies, Mexico witnessed significant growth in trade during the 1990s. The East Asian countries, especially Malaysia, Korea and Philippines, have also rebounded strongly since 2000.

Along with growth in overall volume, the pattern of world trade also underwent changes following structural shifts in production caused by new technologies, demand patterns and new international trade rules under WTO. Primary products and resource-based manufactures have been gradually losing importance with world trade witnessing a shift towards non-resource-based products of increasing technology intensity. In keeping with this trend, there has also been a rapid change in the composition of exports of developing countries from being primary commodity exports to exports of manufactures.

1.2 Trade Openness since 1980s

Trade openness, conventionally measured as the sum of exports and imports of goods as a ratio of GDP, brings out clearly the growing trade liberalisation over time. For most of emerging economies (including India), their openness is much higher than that during the 1980s. This has been facilitated, *inter alia*, by significant reduction in import tariffs. Tariffs have been reduced by more than half in most of the developing countries, including India, since the beginning of the last decade. Despite reductions, tariffs in India remain one of the highest amongst the emerging market economies (EMEs).

In short, the US, East Asian countries and China played a crucial role in expanding world trade in the 1980s. Buoyancy in world trade in the 1990s was sustained despite the lacklustre economic performance of several industrialised countries especially those in Europe and Japan. Although the Asian crisis did cause a major disruption in international trade, the crisis-affected countries have rebounded in recent years with growing trade volumes. Moreover, trade among developing countries has increased significantly in recent years.

1.2.1 Developing Countries and Trade Openness: Present day developing countries, in most cases, have a colonial past marked by extensive exploitation of their economies by the colonial masters. Foreign trade was the chief instrument of this exploitation. Resultantly, many underdeveloped countries of Asia and Africa which achieved independence in the post-Second World War period viewed foreign trade and investment with a certain amount of suspicion. Hence, they focused their attention to the domestic markets. Many of them also adopted economic planning as a tool of rapid industrialisation and agriculture development of their economies in order to reduce their dependence for manufactured goods on the developed countries. This meant emphasis on import substitution (self-reliance) through tariff protection of domestic industries, direct controls on imports and investments, and overvalued exchange rates.

Resultantly, the benefits of buoyant world trade witnessed in the aftermath of the Second World War could not be adequately reaped by a large number of developing countries. Policy makers in several developing countries took a pessimistic view on using international trade as the engine of growth and adopted instead, inward looking development strategies which emphasised import substitution rather than promotion of trade. The negative effect of the inward looking policies on efficiency, productivity and competition set off a process of rethinking among the policy makers in the 1970s.

The situation changed radically when some Asian countries including Japan, South Korea, Singapore, Taiwan, and Hong Kong adopted policies of import liberalisation and export promotion in the 1960s. Consequently, a sizeable number of developing countries, especially from East Asia, opted for more outward looking policies. Over time, these countries transformed themselves from being producers of labour-intensive undifferentiated products to exporters of skill and technology-intensive products. The economic success of many of these countries encouraged other developing countries to increase their trade openness. As a result, since the 1980s, a large number of developing countries have unilaterally increased their openness towards international trade. The liberalisation of merchandise trade and other current account transactions by a large cross-section of countries provided a noticeable thrust to the world trade in the 1990s. Simultaneously, at the multilateral level, the successful conclusion of the Uruguay Round of trade negotiations under the aegis of the General Agreement on Tariffs and Trade (GATT) and the establishment of the World Trade Organisation (WTO) in 1995 created an environment for freer trade.

The remarkable successes of these countries prompted many developing countries including India to rethink in favour of liberalisation of their trade policies. Falling in line with the policies of other Asian countries, India also opted, though somewhat belatedly, for a policy of trade liberalisation beginning 1990s. Since then, trade policy reforms have been introduced to open the Indian economy to the rest of the world with a view to integrate it with the global market. This was an appropriate response to the emerging international economic order, particularly after the establishment of WTO in 1995.

1.3 Emergence of World Trade Organization (WTO)

1.3.1 Establishment of WTO: Created by Uruguay Round of Negotiations (1986-94), WTO was established on January 1, 1995 with headquarters in Geneva, Switzerland. As on August 1, 2018, 164 countries of the world were members of WTO. WTO's creation in 1995 marked the biggest reform of international trade since 1948. During those 47 years, international commerce was regulated under General Agreement on Tariffs and Trade (GATT) which helped establish a prosperous multilateral trading system.

However, by the end of 1980s an overhaul was due.

The Eighth Round of multilateral trade negotiations held under GATT and named Uruguay Round, resulted in new legal agreements for trade and strengthening settlement system. Following this, there was a Ministerial Conference in Marrakesh, Morocco in April 1994 attended by 125 government representatives from across the world to sign for the establishment of a new successor institution of GATT, namely the World Trade Organization (WTO). WTO entered into force on January 1, 1995, with all assets and liabilities of GATT transferred to the former. WTO replaced GATT which remained in existence from 1948 to 1994. GATT was a multilateral treaty, governing trade in goods only. WTO is much wider in scope and coverage.

The Uruguay Round was the largest trade negotiations ever. At times the talks seemed doomed to fail, but in the end the Uruguay Round was successful. The task was so immense that some people wondered whether there would ever be another negotiations like these. Was it the round to end all rounds?

WTO is GATT plus a lot more. GATT (the institution) was small and provisional, and not even recognised in law as international organisation. It was replaced by WTO. GATT (the agreement) was amended and incorporated into the new WTO Agreements. GATT dealt only with trade in goods. WTO Agreements cover services and intellectual property as well.

WTO is the only international body dealing with the rules of trade between nations. At its heart are the WTO agreements, the legal ground rules for international commerce and for trade policy. The agreements have three main objectives: (a) to help trade flow as freely as possible, (b) to achieve further liberalisation gradually through negotiations and (c) to set up an impartial means of settling disputes.

A number of simple, fundamental principles run throughout all the WTO agreements. They are the foundation of the multilateral trading system. They include: non-discrimination, freer trade, predictable policies, encouragement to competition and extra provisions for less developed countries.

The economic case for an open trading system based on multilaterally agreed rules is simple enough and rests largely on commercial common sense. Protectionism leads to bloated inefficient companies and can in the end lead to factory closures and job losses. One of the WTO's objectives is to reduce protectionism.

Broadly speaking, WTO has set to continue negotiations and bring agreements in the following areas.

1. Basic telecommunications.
2. Maritime transport.
3. Movement of natural persons.
4. Financial services.
5. General Agreement on Trade and Services (GATS).
6. A reaffirmation of the rule of law in trade and economic relations.
7. A reversal of long standing protectionist practices in agriculture, textiles and clothing.
8. An extension of multilateral rules to services and intellectual property rights.

WTO is run by its member governments. All major decisions are made by the membership as a whole, either by ministers (who meet every two years) or by officials (who meet regularly in Geneva). Decisions are normally taken by consensus. More routine work is supervised by the General Council. Numerous other councils, committees, working parties and negotiating groups cover the wide range of WTO issues.

WTO is directed by a Ministerial Conference which is the highest authority and meets at least once every two years. So far, 11 Ministerial Conferences have been held: Singapore (December 1996), Geneva (May 1998), Seattle (November-December 1999), Doha (November 2001), Cancun (September 2003), Hong Kong (December 2005), Geneva (November-December 2009), Geneva (December 2011), Bali (December 2013, Nairobi (December 2015) and Buenos Aires (December 2017). The 12th Ministerial Conference would be held in Astana, Kazakhstan in June 2020.

WTO is based on the principles of non-discrimination, free trade and promotion of fair competition among the member countries. About 95 percent of the global trade is governed by the rules and regulations of WTO.

WTO agreements are permanent and ratified by the Parliaments of member countries.

1.3.2 Functions of WTO: WTO performs the following functions:

1. Administering WTO trade agreements.
2. Forum for trade negotiations.
3. Handling trade disputes.
4. Monitoring national trade policies.
5. Technical assistance and training for developing countries.
6. Cooperation with other international organizations.

WTO deals with the global rules of trade between nations. Its main function is to ensure that trade flows as smoothly, predictably and freely as possible.

There are various ways of looking at WTO. It is an organization for trade opening. It is a forum for governments to negotiate trade agreements. It is a place for them to settle trade disputes. It operates a system of trade rules. Essentially, WTO is a place where member governments try to sort out trade problems they face with each other.

WTO was born out of negotiations, and everything the WTO does is the result of negotiations. The bulk of WTO's current work comes from the 1986-94 negotiations called the Uruguay Round and earlier negotiations under the General Agreement on Tariffs and Trade (GATT). WTO is currently host to new negotiations under the Doha Development Agenda launched in 2001.

Where countries have faced trade barriers and wanted them lowered, the negotiations have helped to open markets for trade. However, WTO is not just about opening markets, and in some circumstances its rules support maintaining trade barriers—for example to protect consumers or prevent the spread of disease.

At its heart are the WTO agreements, negotiated and signed by the bulk of the world's trading nations. These documents provide the legal ground rules for international commerce. They are essentially contracts, binding governments to keep their trade policies within agreed limits. Although negotiated and signed by governments, the goal is to help producers of goods and services, exporters, and importers to conduct their business, while allowing governments to meet social and environmental objectives.

The system's overriding purpose is to help trade flow as freely as possible—so long as there are no undesirable side effects—because this is important for economic development and well-being. It partly means removing obstacles. It also means ensuring that individuals, companies and governments know what the trade rules are around the world, and giving them the confidence that there will be no sudden changes of policy. In other words, the rules have to be transparent and predictable.

Trade relations often involve conflicting interests. Agreements, including those painstakingly negotiated in the WTO system, often need interpreting. The most harmonious way to settle these differences is through some neutral procedure based on an agreed legal foundation. That is the purpose behind the dispute settlement process written into the WTO agreements.

While the WTO is driven by its member states, it could not function without its Secretariat to coordinate the activities. The Secretariat employs over 634 staff and its experts—lawyers, economists, statisticians and communications experts—assist WTO members to ensure, among other things, that negotiations progress smoothly, and that the rules of international trade are correctly applied and enforced.

A. Trade Negotiations: WTO agreements cover goods, services and intellectual property. They spell out the principles of liberalization, and the permitted exceptions. They include commitments of individual countries to lower customs tariffs and other trade barriers, and to open and keep open services markets. They set procedures for settling disputes. These agreements are not static; they are renegotiated from time to time and new agreements can be added to the package. Many are now being negotiated under the Doha Development Agenda, launched by WTO trade ministers in Doha, Qatar, in November 2001.

B. Implementation and Monitoring: WTO agreements require governments to make their trade policies transparent by notifying the WTO about laws in force and measures adopted. Various WTO councils and committees seek to ensure that these requirements are being followed and that WTO agreements are being properly implemented. All WTO members must undergo periodic scrutiny of their trade policies and practices, each review containing reports by the country concerned and the WTO Secretariat.

C. Dispute Settlement: WTO's procedure for resolving trade quarrels under the Dispute Settlement Understanding is vital for enforcing the rules and therefore for ensuring that trade flows smoothly. Countries bring disputes to the WTO if they think their rights under the agreements are being infringed. Judgements by specially appointed independent experts are based on interpretations of the agreements and commitments of individual countries.

D. Building Trade Capacity: WTO agreements contain special provision for developing countries, including longer time periods to implement agreements and commitments, measures to increase their trading opportunities, and support to help them build their trade capacity, to handle disputes and to implement technical standards. WTO organizes hundreds of technical cooperation missions to developing countries annually. It also holds numerous courses each year in Geneva for government officials. *Aid for Trade* aims to help developing countries develop the skills and infrastructure needed to expand their trade.

E. Outreach: WTO maintains regular dialogue with non-governmental organizations, parliamentarians, other international organizations, media and the general public on various aspects of WTO and the ongoing Doha negotiations, with the aim of enhancing cooperation and increasing awareness of WTO activities.

1.4 Globalization and International Trade

1.4.1 Meaning of Globalization: Globalization implies widening and deepening integration with the *globe*, i.e. with people and processes abroad. Moreover, at the end of the integrative effort there must lie some concrete benefits for the country, because otherwise the globalization being attempted would not be worth the effort. The trend towards the evolution of a global society is generally thought of in economic terms and in terms of the consequences of the revolution in communication technologies. There is undoubtedly much greater economic integration among the nations of the world today. Globalization is widely seen as the most important factor that could influence economies of nations the world over in the new millennium. The rapid advancement in information technology and communications has made it not just possible but absolutely essential for economies of the world to adapt or fall by the wayside.

1.4.2 Dimensions and Features of Globalization: The 1990s witnessed a paradigm shift towards market-oriented economic policies and a careful dismantling of obstacles in its wake. This has helped the smaller, emerging economies gain access to world markets, emergent technologies and collaborations. This has also given them a window to the developed world and helped them understand the significant role of globalization as an instrument, which could be utilised not just to achieve economic efficiency, but also eradicate poverty.

Globalization has also resulted in the creation of a new business framework. More changes can be expected in the business scenario specifically in terms of openness, adaptiveness and responsiveness. The most important dimensions of economic globalization are: (a) breaking down of national barriers; (b) international spread of trade, financial and production activities and (c) growing power of transnational corporations and international financial institutions in these processes. While economic globalization is a very uneven process, with increased trade and investment being focused in a few countries, almost all countries are greatly affected by this process.

A major feature of globalization is the growing concentration and monopolisation of economic resources and power by transnational corporations and by global financial firms and funds. This process has been termed transnationalisation, in which fewer and fewer transnational corporations are gaining a large and rapidly increasing proportion of world economic resources, production and market shares. Where a multinational company used to dominate the market of a single product, a big transnational company (TNC) now typically produces or trades in an increasing multitude of products, services and sectors. Through mergers and acquisitions, fewer and fewer of these TNCs now control a larger and larger share of the global market, whether in commodities, manufactures or services.

Another feature of the current globalization process is the globalization of national policies and policy-making mechanism. National policies (including economic, social, cultural and technological) that until recently were determined by the States and people within a country have increasingly come under the influence of international agencies and processes or by big private corporations and economic/financial players. This has led to the narrowed ability of governments and people to make choices from options in economic, social and cultural policies.

Most developing countries have seen their independent policy-making mechanism capacity eroded, and have to adopt policies influenced by other entities, which may on balance be detrimental to the countries concerned. The developed countries, where the major economic players reside, and which also control the processes and policies of international economic agencies, are better able to maintain control over their own national policies as well as determine the policies and practices of international institutions and the global system. However, it is also true that the large corporations have taken over a large part of decision-making even in the developed countries, at the expense of the power of the state or political and social leaders.

1.4.3 Globalization and Developing Countries: The issue that concerns developing countries is how one can ensure greater participation of the weaker economies in the global process and what needs to be done to ensure that the course of globalization benefits more people in more countries. The uneven and unequal nature of the present globalization is manifested in the fast growing gap between the rich and poor people of the world and between developed and developing countries; and by the large differences among nations in the distribution of gains and losses.

This imbalance leads to polarisation between countries and groups that gain, and the many countries and groups in society that lose out or are marginalised. Globalization, polarisation, wealth concentration and marginalisation are therefore linked through the same process. In this process, investment resources, growth and modern technology are focused on a few countries, mainly in North America, Europe, Japan and a few East Asian countries. A majority of developing countries are excluded from the process, or are participating in it in marginal ways.

Although the developed world is in a dominant position and has been prepared to use this to further their control of the global economy, the developing countries have not done well in organising themselves to co-ordinate on substantial policy and negotiating positions. The developed countries, on the other hand, are well-organised within their own countries, with well-staffed departments dealing with international trade and finance, and with university academics and private and quasi government think tanks helping to obtain information and map policies and strategies. They also have well-organised associations and lobbies associated with their corporations and financial institutions, which have great influence over the government departments.

On the positive side, globalization has compelled developing countries to improve overall economic management, and make their economies efficient. To get a share of global capital and technology, developing countries have to upgrade their social and economic institutions through administrative, legislative and legal reforms. The quality of governance has to improve to encourage productivity and efficiency. Political stability has to be established. In this context, following lessons can be drawn from East Asian countries:

1. Developing human capital is a basic pre-requisite. Successful globalization and the knowledge economy require educated, healthy and skilled people.
2. It is necessary to build up domestic savings and put them to productive use.
3. Sound economic management and macro-economic balances are necessary. Large fiscal deficit is a serious obstacle to globalization.
4. Good governance at the national and sub-national levels builds confidence among investors.
5. Transparency has to be established in the functioning of both government and business units.
6. Free and open market economies require effective regulatory authorities because role of government changes from control and regulation to governance and facilitation.
7. Modernised capital markets with effective regulatory authorities are necessary to impart confidence to investors by maintaining stability and regulating speculative forces.

1.4.4 Globalization and the Poor: The socio-economically disadvantaged are yet to benefit from globalization. The challenge to overcome the scourge of poverty remains a daunting task. The support of the poor for reforms and their involvement in the development process can be achieved only if they start benefiting from government policies. It is necessary to ensure that the poor and the deprived have a greater stake in economic reforms than at present for mobilising their enthusiastic participation in the development process. Economic reforms must be guided by compassion and distributive justice. Improvement of living conditions of the poorest and the weakest sections of society should be high priority areas of welfare and development programmes/schemes of the government.

1.4.5 Future of Globalization: Globalization is an irreversible trend and developing economies are also inevitably involved in the process. Developed countries should, therefore, carefully consider how to restructure the world trading system to accommodate developing economies, by enabling them to benefit from globalization while minimising external shocks. The World Trade Organization (WTO) should work more effectively, through an enlargement of waiver clauses which recognise the weaker position of developing countries.

Despite distortions and aberrations, globalization is a reality. Developments in information and communication technologies are unifying markets and people, cutting across barriers of space and time. At the end of the day, one has to understand and accept that globalization is the stratagem for the new millennium. Every country, developed and developing, has to accept this and formulate their economies around it.

1.5 Requirements for Robust Growth of World Trade

The nature of world economy, and the role of the governments in it, has undergone a paradigm shift. Driven by an increasingly open and liberalized structure, private sector has matured into a vibrant and dynamic force, operating not just at the international cutting edge, but also with a global scale and reach. This changed economic landscape requires a new administrative paradigm in which the role of government must evolve from simply allocating resources in a command and control economic system, to a far more nuanced one of directing, calibrating, supporting and regulating a market-oriented economic system. Government must thus transition from being a *provider of first and last resort* and *major player* in the economy, to being a *catalyst* nurturing an *enabling environment*, where the entrepreneurial spirits of all, from small self-employed entrepreneurs to large corporations, can flourish.

The world at large has also evolved. Today, we live in a *global village*, connected by modern transport, communications and media, and networked international markets and institutions. In the current global dynamics, a country is also influenced by happenings far removed from its borders.

Recovery in the global economy is proceeding at a modest pace. High political risks and uncertainties pose risks to the fragile recovery. The gradual recovery of growth in the world economy and divergent performances between the countries are due to both structural as well as cyclical factors. Therefore, the appropriate solutions should be nuanced. The dynamics for a strong, sustainable, balanced and inclusive growth will probably remain weak in the foreseeable future. Policy action on four main areas is needed: (a) improving the macroeconomic policy setting, (b) increasing the potential growth rate, (c) making growth inclusive and sustainable and (d) minimizing risks and maximizing benefits of the digital economy.

Recovery in the global economy is proceeding at a modest pace. Six years after the financial and economic crisis, the global output gap is still substantial, the markets continue to be shaky, and the future is overshadowed by severe political risks. Due to high uncertainties, public and private investments remain subdued in most parts of the world.

The pace of recovery varies from one economic region to another. Some economies—such as the United States and the United Kingdom—are above their pre-crisis output levels, while others—such as the Euro zone and Japan—are not. Emerging economies remain the locomotive of global growth, though there are differences among them. Although decelerating, growth is still robust in China, weak in Russia and Brazil while it is strong in India, Indonesia, and South Africa. Oil-producing and exporting countries like Russia, Saudi Arabia, Nigeria, Iran and Venezuela are likely to be adversely affected by sliding crude prices. Conversely, the drop in global oil prices provides a substantial stimulus to the economies of net-oil-importing countries, viz. Turkey, Korea, China, and India.

Global economic growth is threatened by high political risks and uncertainties posed by conflicts in East Europe, North Africa, Middle East, and East Asia. With the demise of the *de-coupling hypothesis,* uncertainties in conflict zones are likely to be transmitted to other economies of the world. In the context of globalization, world economies sink and swim together.

All countries face the same challenge of increasing the pace of job creation and, wherever possible, improving the quality of jobs. Although the situation has improved somewhat, unemployment remains a key concern. Employment in many countries is still far below its pre-2008 levels. Even for people who still have jobs, working conditions have deteriorated. According to the International Labour Organization (ILO), unemployment worldwide has risen by 30 million since the crisis began, currently peaking at 200 million. The average unemployment rate in developed economies stands at 8.5 percent, compared with 5.8 percent before the crisis. In the developing world, unemployment rose only slightly during the crisis, and is now back to pre-crisis levels.

The weak recovery of world economy is also attributable to rising protectionism. According to the WTO, there has been a significant increase in restrictive trade measures introduced by G20 economies since 2008. Import tariffs have remained low but regulatory burdens and non-tariff barriers— including onerous environmental and safety standards—impede international trade. The WTO report on G20 Trade Measures said that, of the 1,244 restrictive measures recorded since the onset of the financial crisis, only 282 have been removed and the number of restrictive measures in place had increased by 12 percent in 2013. Inefficient customs and other border procedures impose unnecessary costs that are transferred to customers.

2

India and Regional Trade Agreements (RTAs)

2.1 Emergence of Regional Trade Agreements (RTAs)

Multilateral trade agreements are the first best solutions for deepening global trade and development as they are founded on the core principles of non-discrimination. RTAs are efforts by nations aimed at deepening economic relations, usually with neighbouring countries, and tend to be largely political in nature. With the multilateral trade negotiations process under the WTO being a painfully slow one requiring broad-based consensus, RTAs have progressively assumed greater importance and a growing share in international trade. While RTAs are broadly compliant with WTO mandates and remain broadly supportive of the WTO process, they remain second-best solutions that are discriminatory in nature against non-members and are inefficient as low cost producing non-members lose out to members.

While bilateral RTAs have no equity considerations, mega-regional trading groups may not necessarily be equitable if membership is diverse and small countries may lose out either way—if they are part of it they may not have much say and if they are not, they may stand to lose.

India has always stood for an open, equitable, predictable, non-discriminatory and rule-based international trading system and views RTAs as building blocks in the overall objective of trade liberalization as well as complementing the multilateral trading system under the WTO.

Bilateral and regional trading arrangements have gradually become permanent features of the global trading architecture. As per WTO statistics, there were 287 Regional Trade Agreements (RTAs) in force as of May 1, 2018. RTAs have clearly become the rule rather than the exception. RTAs are an important means to take advantage of tariff reduction, address non-tariff barriers, facilitate the integration of the economy into global value chains and production networks and also attract investment in potential growth sectors.

With the declining role of tariffs, non-tariff barriers are increasingly becoming more crucial and RTAs provide a potentially effective tool to address such measures.

The need to attract foreign investment for boosting manufacturing and increasing competitiveness, thereby generating employment, is also a consideration for entering into Comprehensive Economic Cooperation Agreements (CECAs) and Comprehensive Economic Partnership Agreements (CEPAs).

What are free trade agreements? These arrangements are known by various nomenclatures such as Preferential Trade Agreements (PTAs), Free Trade Agreements (FTAs), Regional Trade Agreements (RTAs), Comprehensive Economic Cooperation Agreements (CECAs), Comprehensive Economic Partnership Agreements (CEPAs), Broad-based Trade and Investment Agreements (BTIA) etc. The basic difference is in the coverage with CECA/CEPA/BTIA covering an integrated package of agreements on goods (both tariffs and non-tariff barriers), services, investment, intellectual property etc. while the more traditional FTAs are limited to trade in goods.

2.2 India's *Look East* Policy

India has been actively engaging in regional and bilateral trade negotiations with a view to diversifying and expanding the markets for its exports as well as ensuring access to raw materials, intermediates and capital goods for stimulating value added domestic manufacturing.

RTAs are an integral part of India's foreign trade policy, complementing the multilateral trading system. Prior to economic reforms process initiated in 1991, India had adopted a very cautious and guarded approach to regionalism. Recognising that RTAs would continue to feature prominently in world trade, India engaged with its trading partners/blocks with the intention of expanding its export market and began concluding in principle agreements and moving in some cases even towards Comprehensive Economic Cooperation Agreements (CECAs) which cover Free Trade Agreements (FTAs) in goods, services, investments and identified areas of economic cooperation.

Framework agreements have already been entered into with a number of trading partners with specific road maps to be followed and specified time frames by which the negotiations are to be completed. Joint Study Groups have also been set up for examining feasibility of CECAs between India-Japan, India-Brazil-South Africa and India-Russia. India and European Commission have also set up a High Level Trade Group (HLTG) as mandated by the India-EU Summit held in New Delhi on September 7, 2005. The mandate of the HLTG is to explore ways and means to increase bilateral economic flows including the possible launching of negotiations on a comprehensive trade and investment agreement.

India unveiled the *Look East* policy in 1991. East Asia—including Japan, China, South Korea and ASEAN—is today India's largest trading partner, ahead of EU and the US. Proliferation of Free Trade Agreements (FTAs) is the clearest evidence of Asian countries' desire to forge closer economic relationships. The growing importance of CECA's indicates that such agreements are becoming deeper, extending to areas beyond just tariff reduction. Intra-regional trade and investment require building up of shared infrastructure.

Many Asian countries have joined together to develop cross-border infrastructure to lay the foundations for closer trading relationships and increased connectivity among countries. The Greater Mekong Sub-region is quite advanced in this endeavour. Similar initiatives are underway in South Asia and in Central Asia, with exciting prospects for future development. The spirit of enhanced monetary cooperation in Asia is evident from initiatives like the Chiang Mai Initiative and the Asian Bond Fund having major potential for financing regional investments.

Asia remains one of the least integrated regions lacking a continent-wide regional organization. Forging closer links among Asian nations through appropriate institutional mechanisms can lead to substantial enhancement of national, regional and global productivity and output. In the past, India had adopted a very cautious approach to regionalism, and was engaged in only a few bilateral/regional initiatives, mainly through Preferential Trade Agreements (PTAs). Recognising that RTAs would continue to feature in world trade for a long time, and with the intention of expanding its export market, India began concluding in principle agreements as a possible step towards CECAs, which cover FTA in goods (zero customs duty regime within a fixed time frame on items covering substantial trade, and a relatively small negative list of sensitive items with no or limited duty concessions), services, investment and identified areas of economic cooperation.

The CECA with Singapore was implemented from August 1, 2005. The Agreement on South Asia Free Trade Area (SAFTA) was signed by member countries of South Asian Association for Regional Cooperation (SAARC) in January, 2004. Negotiations on all aspects of SAFTA were deliberated and the tariff liberalization programme was implemented from July 1, 2006. Framework Agreement on Comprehensive Economic Cooperation between ASEAN and India, Framework Agreement for Bangladesh, India, Myanmar, Sri Lanka and Thailand Economic Cooperation (BIMSTEC) FTA, and India-Thailand Framework Agreement have also been signed, and FTA on Goods, Services and Investment with BIMSTEC are under negotiation. India-China, India-Japan, and India-South Korea joint study groups have also been set up.

2.3 ASEAN and India

India's engagement with the Association of South East Asian Nations (ASEAN) started with its *Look East Policy* in the year 1991. ASEAN has a membership of 10 countries, namely Brunei Darussalam, Cambodia, Indonesia, Lao PDR,

Malaysia, Myanmar, Philippines, Singapore, Thailand and Vietnam. India became a Sectoral Dialogue Partner of ASEAN in 1992 and Full Dialogue Partner in 1996. In November 2001, the ASEAN-India relationship was upgraded to the summit level.

The First ASEAN Economic Ministers (AEM)-India Consultations were held on September 15, 2002 in Brunei Darussalam where the Ministers, after discussing the Joint Study Report decided to establish an ASEAN-India Economic Linkages Task Force (AIELTF).

The AIELTF was asked to prepare a draft Framework Agreement to enhance the ASEAN-India trade and economic cooperation before the 2nd AEM-India Consultations. Subsequently, at the First ASEAN-India Summit held on November 5, 2002 in Phnom Penh, Cambodia, the Prime Minister of India made the following major announcements:

- India will extend special and differential trade treatment to ASEAN countries, based on their levels of development to improve their market access to India; and
- FTA within 10 years timeframe.

A Framework Agreement on Comprehensive Economic Cooperation between the Association of South East Asian Nations (ASEAN) and India was signed by the Prime Minster of India and the Heads of Nation/Governments of ASEAN members during the Second ASEAN–India Summit on October 8, 2003 in Bali, Indonesia.

The key elements of the Framework Agreement on Comprehensive Economic Cooperation between ASEAN and India cover FTA in goods, services and investment, as well as Areas of Economic Cooperation. The Agreement also provided for an Early Harvest Programme (EHP) which covers areas of Economic Cooperation and a common list of items for exchange of tariff concessions as a confidence building measure.

Presently, the ASEAN-India Trade Negotiating Committee (TNC) is undertaking negotiations for a Comprehensive

Economic Cooperation Agreement (CECA) which includes a Free Trade Area in goods, services and investment. Agreement has been reached on the Rules of Origin and Dispute Settlement Mechanism. The TNC is now negotiating the modalities for tariff reduction and elimination.

On August 13, 2009, India and ASEAN signed the Trade in Goods Agreement under the broader framework of a Comprehensive Economic Cooperation Agreement (CECA) between India and ASEAN. The Trade in Goods Agreement provides for elimination of basic customs duty on 80 percent of the tariff lines accounting for 75 percent of the trade in a gradual manner starting from January 1, 2010.

India has excluded 489 HS 6 digit lines from the list of tariff concessions and 590 HS 6 digit lines from the list of tariff eliminations to address sensitivities in agriculture, textiles, auto, chemicals, crude and refined palm oil, coffee, tea, pepper etc.

Conclusions of negotiations for the Services Agreement and Investment Agreement were announced during the ASEAN-India Commemorative Summit held on 20 December 2012 in New Delhi. The Agreement was signed in September 2014.

2.4 Mega Agreements and India

The three mega agreements that are currently being negotiated—namely the Trans Pacific Partnership (TPP), Trans Atlantic Trade and Investment Partnership (TTIP) and the Regional Comprehensive Economic Partnership (RCEP) —add a completely new dimension to the global trading architecture. The 49 participants in these mega agreements are significant economies both in terms of trade volumes and GDP. Statistics indicate that these countries account for nearly 3/4th of global trade and 4/5th of the global GDP.

There is an overlap of participating countries in the three mega agreements. While the United States is common to the TPP and TTIP, 7 countries, namely Australia, Brunei, Japan, Malaysia, New Zealand, Singapore and Vietnam are part of both the TPP and RCEP.

India is engaged in the RCEP negotiations which are a comprehensive free trade agreement between the 10 ASEAN Member States and ASEAN's FTA (Free Trade Agreement) partners viz. Australia, China, India, Japan, Korea and New Zealand. The 16 RCEP countries cover around 49 percent of world population, 30 percent of global GDP and 29 percent of global trade.

India recognizes the evolution of mega agreements as a significant development in the global trade architecture. These agreements are perceived by some as consequences of the stalemate in the WTO or due to the unique process of decision making in the multilateral institution while others perceive it as a natural progression of ambitions on the part of major players in the WTO.

While India's commitment to the processes and substance of the WTO remains firm, it must also recognize the emerging challenges from the mega agreements under negotiation. These agreements create a significant layer in the global trade architecture for preferential trading among prominent members of the WTO. They also reflect the high ambitions of the participating members in rule making. Tariff reduction is no more a major challenge for these countries. Therefore, rules harmonization, achieving coherence, and removal of non-tariff barriers, are the major tasks that these negotiations intend to address.

Among the 3 agreements, the TPP seems to be at the most advanced stage of development. On account of its position on several matters dictated by the stage of its social and economic development, India cannot be a party to either of these agreements. But they are bound to challenge India's industry in many ways. Firstly, they will erode existing preferences for Indian products in established traditional markets such as the US and EU, benefiting those who are partners to these agreements. Secondly, they are likely to develop a rules architecture which will place a greater burden of compliance on India's manufacturing and services standards for access to the markets of the participating countries. However, these challenges should be treated as an opportunity to respond strategically and to persuade Indian industry to rise to the challenge of higher standards both in the area of products and services, and the framework of rules.

Therefore, the Government should work towards facilitating Indian industry to do so. The RCEP negotiations are on track. Parties to these negotiations are engaged in serious discussions, round after round, on issues of modalities and the extent of liberalisation. India will continue to engage in these negotiations in the right spirit of concluding them in time while taking into account the interest of its business and industry.

2.5 Trans-Pacific Partnership (TPP) and India

TPP agreement is one new mega-regional block that has become a reality and has implication for India.

The 12 Pacific Rim nations (Australia, Brunei, Canada, Chile, Japan, Malaysia, Mexico, New Zealand, Peru, Singapore, the US and Vietnam) signed the TPP agreement on October 5, 2015. It is likely to set higher standards for goods and services trade. It is considered a mega regional FTA which can be a pioneer in many ways.

The TPP is likely to be a game-changer for the world economy and global trade. The 12 members of the TPP account for around 40 percent of global GDP and around 60 percent of merchandise trade. In terms of economic size, the TPP is larger than the existing North America Free Trade Area (NAFTA).

The TPP trade agreement is very comprehensive and not only encompasses the scope of tariff-eliminating mega regional trade pacts, but also aims at setting higher global standards for international trade through lower benchmarks for non-tariff barriers, more stringent labour and environment regulation, higher intellectual property rights (IPR) protection, greater transparency in government procurement and limiting advantages to state-owned enterprises (SoEs) and transparency in health care technology, competitiveness and supply chains. It includes new and emerging trade issues and cross-cutting concerns such as internet and digital economy and participation of SOEs in global trade and investment. In the short-run, the trade impact of the TPP may not be seriously adverse but careful analysis is required for adapting and responding to the challenges in the long run.

According to one estimate [1], India could experience huge export gains of more than US$ 500 billion per year—a 60 percent increase—from joining an expanded TPP or participating in a comprehensive Free Trade Area of the Asia Pacific (FTAAP), now being considered by the Asia-Pacific Economic Cooperation (APEC), and Indian national income would expand by 4 percent (over US$ 200 billion).

The estimates [2] show that India's exports would rise by around US$ 5.3 billion annually; however, imports into India would rise by US$ 10.4 billion, leaving a net deficit in balance of trade of US$ 5.1 billion. India is most competitive in services trade and reduction of trade barriers in services among TPP members will result in growth in India's services exports.

The possible risks of not joining the TPP are difficult to quantify, but some of the research has highlighted the possibility of trade diversion and raised concerns about erosion of India's share in exports to the US and Europe. TPP is expected to make around 11,000 tariff lines duty free for its members, which may result in loss of competitiveness of Indian exports in these markets.

This will lower India's export share to the US and the EU, shifting it to the TPP developing countries instead. Some of the export sectors such as textiles and clothing industry are likely to face stiff competition from Vietnam, and it may lead to trade diversion. However, the implementation of stringent non-tariff measures is likely to increase the cost of production and will erode the competitiveness of exports of TPP member countries which will reduce the extent of trade diversion from India. There is also the concern of investment diversion, particularly as countries like Vietnam would offer more robust investor protection.

Some analysts have cautioned that India has to give due consideration to the costs if it is desirous of joining the TPP, as it will be required to comply with provisions relating to tariffs, SoEs, agriculture and IPR protection. Some of the major concerns are as follows:

2.5.1 Import Competition: Domestic industries will face severe import competition due to tariff elimination on some of the products. Indian industry is already battling infrastructure deficiency and implementation of stringent measures may raise the cost of production, threatening the survival of domestic manufacturing.

2.5.2 State-owned Enterprises (SoEs): Membership of the TPP would prevent the government from using SoEs and government procurement as vehicles for achieving social and economic objectives, including employment generation. India would have to compromise on the Make in India policy.

2.5.3 Intellectual Property Rights (IPRs): The TPP agreement on IPRs does not prevent a party from taking measures to protect public health and, in particular, to promote access to medicines for all. However, the prices of pharmaceutical products can be expected to rise due to implementation of IPR agreements which will give more protection to patented medicine and may lead substantially to elimination of generic drugs from the market. Nobel laureate Joseph Stiglitz has expressed concern that 'the efforts to raise drug prices in the TPP take us in the wrong direction. The whole world may come to pay a price in the form of worse health and unnecessary deaths'. Implementation of patent term adjustment rules significantly delays entry of generic medicines and restricts access to affordable medicines.

2.5.4 Government Procurement: Apart from stressing non-discriminatory, fair and transparent procurement procedures, the TPP specifies timely publication of complete information on the procuring entity, the specific procurement, the time frame for submission of bids, and a description of conditions for participation of suppliers. As the agreement curtails the flexibility available to signatory countries to impose export restrictions on food, it will jeopardize India's endeavour to ensure food security.

2.5.5 Labour Standards: TPP has gone beyond core labour standards to include *acceptable conditions of work* within its ambit. These bind the members to adopt and maintain laws and practices governing acceptable conditions of work relating to minimum wages, hours of work, and occupational health and safety determined by each party. These labour standards may increase the labour cost in the developing countries as they raise the issue of enforceable commitments which require the member countries to pass legislation in line with the TPP labour standard and put effective implementation agencies in place.

2.5.6 Environment Standard in TPP Agreement: The TPP agreement goes beyond the provisions in other FTAs to include new ones that will address wildlife trafficking, illegal logging and illegal fishing practices. The TPP members acknowledge that inadequate fisheries management, fisheries subsidies that contribute to over-fishing and overcapacity, and illegal, unreported and unregulated (IUU) fishing can have significant negative impacts on trade, development and the environment and 'thus recognize the need for individual and collective action to address the problems of over-fishing and unsustainable utilization of fisheries resources'. This is in contradiction to India's current policy of subsidizing the fishery industry. It may severely affect special governmental assistance programmes for around 15 million poor fishermen in India. Fishery subsidies rule has been incorporated for the first time in an FTA agreement and this will set the standard for other countries in the WTO arena.

Hence, these TPP rules are likely to affect the multilateral process and impact India, independently of whether it joins the TPP or not.

2.6 WTO's Stand on RTAs

Since deadlock is persisting in trade negotiations due to difference between developed countries and developed countries on certain issues, the developed countries are gradually adopting a new strategy. The developed countries are adamant on certain issues that are core to the interest of developing countries. Developed countries are developing plurilateral agreements outside WTO, which may render the WTO only a dispute settlement body.

The diplomatic statements and division in opinions indicates end of the development round for developing countries. Developed countries are reluctant to resolve the problem of distortions in global agricultural trade. Negotiations on services have been put to back burners, also harming the interest of developing countries in professional services.

In response, the developing countries should prepare their strategy. First, the developing countries should stick to the traditional multilateral approach to expand and conclude trade negotiations as envisaged in the WTO based on decisions and discussions among the WTO Members, including the Doha Development Agenda.

Second, simultaneously, developing countries may allow plurilateral to multilateral approach or the new possibility developed by some developed countries consequent upon deadlock in WTO talks since 2008, first initiating the plurilateral agreements and then making efforts to bring them within the WTO framework and, simultaneously, forming free trade agreements and bilateral trade agreements. The failure of the Ministerial Conferences might eventually lead to spurt in free trade agreements and bilateral agreements among the countries, especially developed countries, that started being formed for the last four or five years.

According to Article IX (3) of the Marrakesh Agreement, the incorporation of plurilateral agreements into the body of the WTO would require a three-fourth affirmative vote of all

Members. In this way, plurilaterals, once brought in the WTO framework, would restore the WTO as the principal global forum for addressing new issues. However, this is a tough task.

They seem to be contradictory, but often regional trade agreements can actually support the WTO's multilateral trading system. Regional agreements have allowed groups of countries to negotiate rules and commitments that go beyond what was possible at the time multilaterally. In turn, some of these rules have paved the way for agreement in the WTO. Services, intellectual property, environmental standards, investment and competition policies are all issues that were raised in regional negotiations and later developed into agreements or topics of discussion in the WTO.

The groupings that are important for the WTO are those that abolish or reduce barriers on trade within the group. The WTO agreements recognize that regional arrangements and closer economic integration can benefit countries. It also recognizes that under some circumstances regional trading arrangements could hurt the trade interests of other countries. Normally, setting up a customs union or free trade area would violate the WTO's principle of equal treatment for all trading partners ("most-favoured-nation"). However, GATT's Article 24 allows regional trading arrangements to be set up as a special exception, provided certain strict criteria are met. In particular, the arrangements should help trade flow more freely among the countries in the group without barriers being raised on trade with the outside world. In other words, regional integration should complement the multilateral trading system and not threaten it.

Article 24 says if a free trade area or customs union is created, duties and other trade barriers should be reduced or removed on substantially all sectors of trade in the group. Non-members should not find trade with the group any more restrictive than before the group was set up.

Similarly, Article 5 of the General Agreement on Trade in Services provides for economic integration agreements in services. Other provisions in the WTO agreements allow developing countries to enter into regional or global agreements that include the reduction or elimination of tariffs and non-tariff barriers on trade among themselves.

On February 6, 1996, the WTO General Council created the Regional Trade Agreements Committee. Its purpose is to examine regional groups and to assess whether they are consistent with WTO rules. The committee is also examining how regional arrangements might affect the multilateral trading system, and what the relationship between regional and multilateral arrangements might be.

Endnotes

1. Bergsten, Fred C. (2015), "India's Rise: A Strategy for Trade-led Growth", Trade and Investment Policy Watch, Petersons Institute for International Economics (PIIE) Briefing, 15-4, September.
2. Banga, R. and Sahu, P.K. (2015), "Trans-Pacific Partnership Agreement (TPPA): Implications for India's Trade and Investments", Centre for WTO Studies, Indian Institute of Foreign Trade, Working Paper No. SWS/wp/200/2014, October.

3

ASEAN: An Overview

ASEAN is a regional inter-governmental organization comprising of ten Southeast Asian countries that promotes inter-governmental co-operation and facilitates economic, political, security, military, educational and socio-cultural integration amongst its members and other Asian states. The ten member countries are: Indonesia, Singapore, Philippines, Malaysia, Brunei Darussalam, Thailand, Cambodia, Lao PDR, Myanmar and Vietnam.

3.1 Establishment of ASEAN

ASEAN regularly engages with other states in the Asia-Pacific region and beyond. Being a global powerhouse, the central platform for cooperation in Asia-Pacific, and one of the world's most prominent and influential organisations, ASEAN maintains a global network of alliances and is involved in numerous international affairs. It is a major partner of the Shanghai Cooperation Organisation (SCO), developing cooperation model with the organisation for peace, stability, development and sustainability of the Asian continent. It also serves as an international role model in seeking harmony and strength among diversity and differences, as well as a leading figure in international diplomacy.

ASEAN was preceded by an organization formed on July 31, 1961 called the Association of Southeast Asia (ASA), a group consisting of the Philippines, Federation of Malaya, and Thailand. ASEAN itself was created on August 8, 1967, when the foreign ministers of five countries, namely Indonesia, Malaysia, the Philippines, Singapore, and Thailand, signed the ASEAN Declaration. As set out in the Declaration, the aims and purposes of ASEAN are to accelerate economic growth, social progress, and cultural development in the region, to promote regional peace, collaboration and mutual assistance on matters of common interest, to provide assistance to each other in the form of training and research facilities, to collaborate for better utilisation of agriculture and industry to raise the living standards of the people, to promote Southeast Asian studies and to maintain close, beneficial co-operation with existing international organisations with similar aims and purposes.

The creation of ASEAN was motivated by a common fear of communism—ASEAN achieved greater cohesion in the mid-1970s following a change in balance of power after the end of the Vietnam War. The region's dynamic economic growth during the 1970s strengthened the organization, enabling ASEAN to adopt a unified response to Vietnam's invasion of Cambodia in 1979. ASEAN's first summit meeting, held in Bali, Indonesia in 1976, resulted in an agreement on several industrial projects and the signing of a Treaty of Amity and Cooperation, and a Declaration of Concord. The end of the Cold War between the United States and the Soviet Union at the end of the 1980s allowed ASEAN countries to exercise greater political independence in the region, and in the 1990s, ASEAN emerged as a leading voice on regional trade and security issues.

3.2 Expansion of ASEAN

In 1984, Brunei became ASEAN's sixth member and on July 28, 1995, Vietnam joined as the seventh member. Laos and Myanmar (Burma) joined two years later on July 23, 1997. Cambodia would have joined at the same time as Laos and Burma, but its entry was delayed due to the country's internal political struggle. It later joined on April 30, 1999, following the stabilization of its government.

On December 15, 1995, the Southeast Asian Nuclear-Weapon-Free Zone Treaty was signed with the intention of turning Southeast Asia into a nuclear weapon free zone. The Treaty took effect on March 28, 1997 after all but one of the member states had ratified it. It became fully effective on June 21, 2001 after the Philippines ratified it, effectively banning all nuclear weapons in the region.

On December 15, 2008, member states met in Jakarta to launch a charter, signed in November 2007, with the aim of moving closer to "an EU-style community". The charter turned ASEAN into a legal entity and aimed to create a single free-trade area for the region encompassing 500 million people.

President of Indonesia Susilo Bambang Yudhoyono stated: "This is a momentous development when ASEAN is consolidating, integrating, and transforming itself into a community. It is achieved while ASEAN seeks a more vigorous role in Asian and global affairs at a time when the international system is experiencing a seismic shift". Referring to climate change and economic upheaval, he concluded: "Southeast Asia is no longer the bitterly divided, war-torn region it was in the 1960s and 1970s".

The financial crisis of 2007-2008 was seen as a threat to the goals envisioned by the charter, and also set forth the idea of a proposed human rights body to be discussed at a future summit in February 2009. This proposition caused controversy, as the body would not have the power to impose sanctions or punish countries which violated citizens' rights and would therefore be limited in effectiveness. The body was established later in 2009 as the ASEAN Intergovernmental Commission on Human Rights (AICHR). In November 2012, the Commission adopted the ASEAN Human Rights Declaration.

3.3 Political Security

ASEAN member states recognise the importance of strengthening food security to maintain stability and prosperity in the region. The World Food Summit of 1996 defined food security as existing: "when all people at all times have access to sufficient, safe, and nutritious food to maintain a healthy and active lifestyle". As ASEAN moves towards AEC and beyond, food security should be an integral part of the ASEAN community building agenda and deserves more attention.

During the 14th ASEAN Summit, the group adopted the ASEAN Political Security Community (APSC) blueprint. This document was aimed at creating a robust political-security environment within ASEAN, with programs and activities outlined to establish the APSC by 2016. The document was based on the principles and purposes of the ASEAN charter, the ASEAN Security Community Plan of Action, the Vientiane Action Program, and other relevant decisions. The APSC aimed to create a rules-based community of shared values and norms, a cohesive, peaceful, stable and resilient region with a shared responsibility toward comprehensive security and a dynamic and outward-looking region in an increasingly integrated and interdependent world.

3.4 Defence Industry Collaboration

The ASEAN Defence Industry Collaboration (ADIC) was proposed at the 4th ASEAN Defence Ministers' Meeting on May 11, 2010 in Hanoi. The emergence of this concept was triggered by the fact that the majority of member states are regular importers of defence products. One of the purposes of this concept was to reduce defence imports from non-ASEAN countries by half and to further develop the defence industry in the region. It was formally adopted during the 5th ASEAN Defence Ministers' Meeting (ADMM) on May 19, 2011, in Jakarta, Indonesia, in line with the ADMM agreement to enhance security co-operation in maritime security, humanitarian assistance and disaster relief, counter-terrorism, and military medicine.

The main focus was to industrially and technologically boost the security capability of ASEAN, consistent with the principles of flexibility and non-binding and voluntary participation among the member states. The concept revolves around education and capability building programs to develop the skills and capabilities of manpower, sharing in the production of capital for defence equipment, components, and spares, and the provision of repair and maintenance services to address all the defence and security needs of each ASEAN country.

It also aimed to develop the defence trade by encouraging member states to participate in the intra-ASEAN defence trade and support trade shows and exhibitions. ADIC aimed to establish a strong defence industry relying on the local capabilities of each member state, and limit annual procurement from original equipment manufacturers (OEMs) outside the region. Countries like US, Germany, Russia, France, Italy, UK, China, South Korea, Israel, and the Netherlands are among the major suppliers to ASEAN.

However, there are challenges to the defence collaboration, namely the unequal level of capabilities among the member states in defence industry, and the lack of established defence trade among them. Prior to the adoption of the ADIC concept, the status of the defence industry base in each of the member states was at disparate level. Singapore, Malaysia, Indonesia, and Thailand were among the top member states with an established defence industry base, but they possess different levels of capacity, while the remaining member states like the Philippines, Laos, Vietnam, Myanmar, and Cambodia have yet to develop and enhance their capabilities in this aspect.

Of the ten member states, Indonesia and Singapore are among the most competitive players. Indonesia is the only member state recognised as one of the top 100 global defence suppliers from 2010-2013. ASEAN member states purchase virtually no defence products from within the ASEAN.

3.5 Counter-terrorism

ASEAN Convention on Counter-Terrorism (ACCT) serves as a framework for regional co-operation to counter, prevent, and suppress terrorism and deepen counter-terrorism co-operation. It was signed by ASEAN leaders in 2007. On April 28, 2011, Brunei ratified the convention and a month later, the convention came into force. Malaysia became the tenth member state to ratify ACCT on January 11, 2013.

3.6 Socio-Cultural Community Blueprint

It was also during the 14th ASEAN Summit that the member governments of ASEAN adopted the ASEAN Socio-Cultural Community (ASCC) blueprint. The ASCC envisions an "ASEAN Community that is people-centred and socially responsible with a view to achieving enduring solidarity and unity among the countries and people of ASEAN by forging a common identity and building a caring and sharing society which is inclusive and harmonious where the well-being, livelihood, and welfare of the peoples are enhanced". Among its focus areas are: human development, social welfare and protection, social justice and rights, ensuring environmental sustainability, building the ASEAN identity, and narrowing the development gap.

3.7 Narrowing the Development Gap (NDG)

NDG is the framework for addressing disparities among, and within, member states where pockets of underdevelopment exist. Under NDG, ASEAN has continued co-ordinating closely with other sub-regional co-operation frameworks, viewing them as "equal partners in the development of regional production and distribution networks" in the AEC, and as a platform to "mainstream social development issues in developing and implementing projects", in the context of the ASCC. The six-year Initiative for ASEAN Integration (IAI) Work Plans have been developed to assist Cambodia, Laos, Myanmar, Vietnam as well as ASEAN's other sub-regions to ensure that the wheels of their economies move at an accelerated pace.

The ASEAN Secretariat, in particular through the IAI and NDG Division, supports the implementation and management of the IAI Work Plan and coordinates activities related to sub-regional frameworks. This includes servicing meetings, assisting in the formulation, implementation, monitoring and reporting of projects, resource mobilisation, and overall operational co-ordination among various IAI and NDG-related stakeholders. The Division works closely with the dialogue partners, and international agencies, to develop strategies and programs to assist in promoting and implementing IAI and NDG activities in ASEAN.

ASEAN's planned integration has challenged its citizens to embrace a regional identity. The call for ASEAN identity delivers a challenge to construct dynamic institutions and foster sufficient amounts of social capital. The underlying assumption is that the creation of a regional identity is of special interest to ASEAN and the intent of the 2020 Vision policy document was to reassert the belief in a regional framework designed as an action plan related to human development and civic empowerment. Accordingly, these assumptions will be the basis for recommendations and strategies in developing a participatory regional identity.

3.8 Free Trade

Free trade initiatives in ASEAN are spearheaded by the implementation of the ASEAN Trade in Goods Agreement (ATIGA) and the Agreement on Customs. These agreements are supported by several sector bodies to plan and to execute free trade measures, guided by the provisions and the requirements of ATIGA and the Agreement on Customs. They form a backbone for achieving targets of the AEC Blueprint and establishing the ASEAN Economic Community by the end of 2015. On August 26, 2007, ASEAN stated its aims of completing free trade agreements (FTAs) with China, Japan, South Korea, India, Australia, and New Zealand by 2013, which is in line with the start of the ASEAN Economic Community by 2015.

In November 2007, ASEAN states signed the ASEAN Charter, a constitution governing relations among member states and establishing the group itself as an international legal entity. During the same year, the Cebu Declaration on East

Asian Energy Security was signed by ASEAN and the other members of the EAS (Australia, China, India, Japan, New Zealand, and South Korea), which pursues energy security by finding energy alternatives to conventional fuels.

On February 27, 2009, an FTA with Australia and New Zealand was signed. It is believed that this FTA would boost combined GDP across the 12 countries by more than US$ 48 billion over the period between 2000 and 2020. Bilateral trade with India crossed the US$ 70 billion target in 2012 (target was to reach the level only by 2015). The agreement with China created the ASEAN-China Free Trade Area (ACFTA), which went into full effect on January 1, 2010. In addition, ASEAN is currently negotiating an FTA with the European Union. Taiwan has also expressed interest in an agreement with ASEAN but needs to overcome diplomatic objections from China. ASEAN, together with its six major trading partners (Australia, China, India, Japan, New Zealand, and South Korea), began the first round of negotiations on February 26-28, 2013, in Bali, Indonesia on the establishment of the RCEP, which is an extension of ASEAN Plus Three and Six that covers 45 percent of the world's population and about a third of the world's total GDP.

3.9 Foreign Relations

ASEAN has been credited as one of the world's most successful and influential organisations, and a global powerhouse. It received high praises from world leaders and the international community, and is dubbed as the centrality in the political, economic, security and socio-cultural architecture of the Asia-Pacific.

It is lauded as the "best-established intergovernmental institution in Asia" while achieving high approval ratings in its own region. Throughout history, ASEAN has formed alliances around the world, and established cooperation and dialogues among countries and sub-regional, regional and international organisations and institutions, solidifying itself as one of the biggest players on the international stage. It also serves as an international role model in seeking harmony and strength among diversity and differences.

Being one of the world's forefront political, economic and security meetings, the ASEAN Summit serves as a prominent regional (Asia) and international (worldwide) conference, with world leaders attending its related summits and meetings to discuss about various problems and global issues, strengthening cooperation, and making decisions. The summit has been praised by world leaders for its success and ability to produce results on a global level.

However, despite its international success, recognition and influence, ASEAN still received several criticisms. Critics have charged that ASEAN is too soft in its approach in promoting human rights and democracy, particularly in junta-led Burma. Some scholars think that non-interference has hindered ASEAN's efforts to handle the Burma issue, human rights abuse, and haze pollution in the area. Despite global outrage at the military crackdown on unarmed protesters in Yangon, ASEAN has refused to suspend Burma as a member, and also rejected proposals for economic sanctions.

This has caused concern as the European Union has refused to conduct free trade negotiations at a regional level for these political reasons. During a UN vote against the ethnic cleansing of Rohingya, a majority of member states voted to either abstain or were against the condemnation. Only Muslim-majority countries Malaysia, Indonesia, and Brunei voted in favour of condemning the cleansing of Rohingya. Some international observers view ASEAN as a "talk shop", stating that the organisation is "big on words, but small on action".

4

India-ASEAN Relations and the Delhi Declaration of January 25, 2018

Association of Southeast Asian Nations (ASEAN) comprises of Indonesia, Singapore, Philippines, Malaysia, Brunei, Thailand, Cambodia, Lao PDR, Myanmar and Vietnam.

India's focus on a strengthened and multi-faceted relationship with ASEAN is an outcome of the significant changes in the world's political and economic scenario since the early 1990s and India's own march towards economic liberalisation. India's search for economic space resulted in the 'Look East Policy'. The Look East Policy has today matured into a dynamic and action-oriented 'Act East Policy. Prime Minister at the 12th ASEAN India Summit and the 9th East Asia Summit held in Nay Pyi Taw, Myanmar, in November 2014, formally enunciated the Act East Policy.

India's relationship with ASEAN is a key pillar of foreign policy and the foundation of our Act East Policy. The upgradation of the relationship into a strategic partnership in 2012 was a natural progression to the ground covered since India became a Sectoral Partner of the ASEAN in 1992, Dialogue Partner in 1996 and Summit Level Partner in 2002. There are, in total, 30 Dialogue Mechanisms between India and ASEAN, cutting across various sectors. India has set up a separate Mission to ASEAN and the EAS in Jakarta in April 2015 with a dedicated ambassador to strengthen engagement with ASEAN and ASEAN-centric processes.

4.1 India's Multilateral Engagement with ASEAN

As a reflection of the interest of ASEAN and India to intensify their engagement, the ASEAN-India Partnership for Peace, Progress and Shared Prosperity, which sets out the roadmap for long-term ASEAN-India engagement, was signed at the 3rd ASEAN-India Summit in 2004 in Vientiane. A Plan of Action (POA) for the period 2004-2010 was also developed to implement the Partnership. The 3rd POA (2016-2020) was adopted by the ASEAN-India Foreign Ministers' meeting held in August 2015 in Kuala Lumpur, Malaysia. Furthermore, ASEAN and India have identified priority areas for the period of 2016-2018 and are already implementing activities under it, which would contribute towards successful implementation of the 2016-2020 Plan of Action.

4.1.1 Political Security Co-operation: Faced with growing traditional and non-traditional challenges, politico-security cooperation is a key and an emerging pillar of our relationship. Rising export of terror, growing radicalization through ideology of hatred, and spread of extreme violence define the landscape of common security threats to our societies. Our partnership with ASEAN seeks to craft a response that relies on coordination, cooperation and sharing of experiences at multiple levels.

The main forum for ASEAN security dialogue is the ASEAN Regional Forum (ARF). India has been attending annual meetings of this forum since 1996 and has actively participated in its various activities. The ASEAN Defence Ministers' Meeting (ADMM) is the highest defence consultative and cooperative mechanism in ASEAN. The ADMM+ brings together Defence Ministers from the 10 ASEAN nations plus Australia, China, India, Japan, New Zealand, Republic of Korea, Russia, and the United States on a biannual basis. Defence Minister attended the 4th ADMM Plus held from October 23-27, 2017 in Manila, Philippines.

4.1.2 Economic Co-operation: India-ASEAN trade and investment relations have been growing steadily, with ASEAN being India's fourth largest trading partner. India's trade with ASEAN has increased to US$ 71.69 billion in 2016-17 from US$ 65 billion in 2015-16. India's export to ASEAN has increased to US$ 31 billion in 2016-17 from US$ 25 billion in 2015-16.

Investment flows are also substantial both ways, with ASEAN accounting for approximately 12.5 percent of investment flows into India since 2000. FDI inflows into India from ASEAN between April 2000 to May 2016 was about US$ 49.40 billion, while FDI outflows from India to ASEAN countries from April 2007 to March 2015, as per data maintained by DEA, was about US$ 38.672 billion. The ASEAN-India Free Trade Area has been completed with the entering into force of the ASEAN-India Agreements on Trade in Service and Investments on July 1, 2015.

ASEAN and India have been also working on enhancing private sector engagement. ASEAN India-Business Council (AIBC) was set up in March 2003 in Kuala Lumpur as a forum to bring key private sector players from India and the ASEAN countries on a single platform for business networking and sharing of ideas.

4.1.3 Socio-Cultural Co-operation: India has been organizing a large number of programmes to boost People-to-People Interaction with ASEAN, such as inviting ASEAN students to India each year for the Students Exchange Programme, Special Training Course for ASEAN diplomats, Exchange of Parliamentarians, Participation of ASEAN students in the National Children's Science Congress, ASEAN-India Network of Think Tanks, ASEAN-India Eminent Persons Lecture Series, etc.

4.1.4 Connectivity: ASEAN-India connectivity is a priority for India as also the ASEAN countries. In 2013, India became the third dialogue partner of ASEAN to initiate an ASEAN Connectivity Coordinating Committee-India Meeting. While India has made considerable progress in implementing the India-Myanmar-Thailand Trilateral Highway and the Kaladan Multimodal Project, issues related to increasing the maritime and air connectivity between ASEAN and India and transforming the corridors of connectivity into economic corridors are under discussion.

A possible extension to India-Myanmar-Thailand Trilateral

Highway to Cambodia, Lao PDR and Vietnam is also under consideration. A consensus on finalising the proposed protocol of the India-Myanmar-Thailand Motor Vehicle Agreement (IMT MVA) has been reached. This agreement will have a critical role in realizing seamless movement of passenger, personal and cargo vehicles along roads linking India, Myanmar and Thailand. The PM announced a line of credit of US$ 1 billion to promote projects that support physical and digital connectivity between India and ASEAN and a Project Development Fund with a corpus of ₹ 500 crore to develop manufacturing hubs in CLMV countries at the 13th ASEAN India Summit held in Malaysia in November 2015.

4.1.5 ASEAN-India Fund: At the 7th ASEAN-India Summit in 2009, India announced a contribution of US$ 50 million to the ASEAN-India Fund, to support implementation of the ASEAN-India Plans of Action, which envisage cooperation in a range of sectors in the political, economic and socio-cultural spheres for deepening and intensifying ASEAN-India cooperation. Projects worth approximately US$ 48 million are under various stages of implementation or processing. In order to take the development and capacity building initiatives forward, PM has proposed enhancing the ASEAN-India Fund with an additional grant of US$ 50 million at the 14th ASEAN India Summit in Vientiane in September 2016.

4.1.6 ASEAN-India S&T Development Fund: At the 6th ASEAN-India Summit in November 2007 in Singapore, India announced the setting up of an ASEAN-India Science and Technology Development Fund with a US$ 1 million contribution from India to promote joint collaborative R&D research projects in science and technology. This Fund become operational in 2009-10 and expenditure began to be incurred from 2010-11. This fund has been enhanced to US$ 5 million from 2016-17. Projects worth US$ 0.67 million are already under implementation and new projects are being identified.

4.1.7 ASEAN-India Green Fund: At the 6th ASEAN-India Summit on November 21, 2007 in Singapore, India announced the setting up of an ASEAN-India Green Fund with an initial contribution of US$ 5 million from India, to support collaboration activities relating to environment and climate change. Some of the areas identified for collaboration under the Fund are climate change, energy efficiency, clean technologies, renewable energy, biodiversity conservation and environmental education. Projects worth US$ 1.97 million covered under this Fund are currently at the implementation stage.

4.1.8 ASEAN-India Projects: India has been cooperating with ASEAN by way of implementation of various projects in the fields of agriculture, science and technology, space, environment and climate change, human resource development, capacity building, new and renewable energy, tourism, people-to-people contacts and connectivity etc. Some of the prominent projects, which are either ongoing or completed are as follows.

Space project envisaging establishment of a tracking, data reception/data processing station in Ho Chi Minh City, Vietnam and upgradation of telemetry tracking and command station in Biak, Indonesia; setting up of centres of excellence in software development and training in CLMV countries; e-network for provision of tele-medicine and tele-education in CLMV countries, quick impact projects in CLMV etc.

Apart from the above projects, India has been supporting ASEAN, especially CLMV countries under the Initiatives for ASEAN Integration, which include projects on training of English language for law enforcement officers in CLMV countries and Training of professionals dealing with capital markets in CLMV by National Institute of Securities Management, Mumbai, scholarships for ASEAN students for higher education at Nalanda University, training of ASEAN civil servants in drought management, disaster risk management, sustainable ground water management etc. To boost people-to-people interaction with ASEAN, India has been organising various programmes including training programme for ASEAN diplomats, exchange of parliamentarians, participation of ASEAN students in the National Children's Science Congress, ASEAN-India Network of Think Tanks, ASEAN-India Eminent Persons Lecture Series, ASEAN-India Students Exchange programme, ASEAN-India Media Exchange programme etc.

In agriculture, India is cooperating with ASEAN by way of projects such as Exchange of Farmers, ASEAN-India Fellowships for Higher Agricultural Education in India and ASEAN, Exchange of Agriculture Scientists, Empowerment of Women through Cooperatives, Training Course on Organic Certification for Fruits and Vegetables etc. In the S&T field, we have projects such as ASEAN-India S&T Digital Library, ASEAN-India Virtual Institute for Intellectual Property, ASEAN-India Collaborative Project on S&T for Combating Malaria, ASEAN-India Programme on Quality Systems in Manufacturing, ASEAN-India Collaborative R&D Project on Mariculture, Bio-mining and Bioremediation Technologies etc.

4.1.9 ASEAN-India Centre (AIC): Set up in 2013, the AIC has been serving as a resource centre for ASEAN Member States and India, for strengthening ASEAN-India strategic partnership and promoting India-ASEAN dialogue and cooperation in the areas of mutual interests. AIC has provided inputs to policy makers in India and ASEAN on implementation of ASEAN-India connectivity initiatives by organising seminars, roundtables etc. AIC also organizes workshops, seminars and conferences on various issues relevant to ASEAN-India strategic partnership. It undertakes regular networking activities with relevant public/private agencies, organizations and think tanks in India and ASEAN and EAS countries, with the aim of providing up-to-date information, data resources and sustained interaction, for promoting ASEAN-India Strategic Partnership.

4.1.10 ASEAN Studies Centre: Inaugurated on August 8, 2016, it functions from the Indian Council of Social Science and Research-North Eastern Regional Centre located in the North-Eastern Hill University (NEHU) in Shillong. The Centre is expected to facilitate ASEAN-India research projects, studies, workshops and related activities.

4.2 Delhi Declaration of the ASEAN-India Commemorative Summit to Mark the 25th Anniversary of ASEAN-India Dialogue Relations

We, the Heads of State/Government of the Member States of the Association of Southeast Asian Nations (ASEAN) and the Republic of India, have gathered in New Delhi, India, on January 25, 2018 to commemorate the 25th Anniversary of ASEAN-India Dialogue Relations under the theme of "Shared Values, Common Destiny";

Reaffirming our commitment to guide ASEAN-India Dialogue Relations by the principles, purposes, shared values and norms enshrined in the Charter of the United Nations, the Treaty of Amity and Cooperation in Southeast Asia (TAC), the Declaration of the East Asia Summit on the Principles for Mutually Beneficial Relations, and the Vision Statement adopted at the ASEAN-India Commemorative Summit to mark the 20th Anniversary of ASEAN-India Dialogue Relations on 20 December 2012; and supporting the ASEAN Charter;

Noting the cross-cultural exchanges and civilisational linkages between Southeast Asia and India over several millennia as a strong foundation for cooperation between ASEAN and India in an increasingly inter-connected world;

Recognising with appreciation the achievements made over the past 25 years of ASEAN-India Dialogue Relations across the three ASEAN Community pillars, namely political-security, economic and socio-cultural;

Noting with satisfaction the progress in the implementation of the Plan of Action to Implement the ASEAN-India Partnership for Peace, Progress and Shared Prosperity (2016-2020) and the List of Priorities for 2016-2018 to implement the ASEAN-India Plan of Action;

Appreciating India's support for ASEAN centrality in the evolving regional architecture and its continued contribution to regional peace, security, and prosperity and to ASEAN integration and the ASEAN Community building process, including through the support for implementation of ASEAN 2025: Forging Ahead Together, Master Plan on ASEAN Connectivity (MPAC) 2025, and the Initiative for ASEAN Integration (IAI) Work Plan III;

Commending various commemorative activities held in ASEAN Member States and India throughout 2017 and the beginning of 2018, which brought the ASEAN-India Strategic Partnership to our communities, including the youth through hosting of the ASEAN-India Youth Summit, the ASEAN-India Youth Awards and Youth Leadership Programme, and ASEAN-India Music Festival;

Hereby agree to the following:

1. Further strengthen and deepen the ASEAN-India Strategic Partnership for mutual benefit, across the whole spectrum of political-security, economic, socio-cultural and development cooperation, through further strengthening of relevant institutional mechanisms and broadening of the network between government institutions, parliamentarians, business circles, scientists, academicians, think tanks, media, youth and other stakeholders, for the building of a peaceful, harmonious, caring and sharing community in our regions.

2. Continue to exert efforts and cooperate towards the full, effective and timely implementation of the Plan of Action to Implement the ASEAN-India Partnership for Peace, Progress and Shared Prosperity (2016-2020).

3. Further enhance high-level engagement and cooperation within the existing framework of the ASEAN-India Dialogue Partnership and ASEAN-led mechanisms, such as the ASEAN-India Summit, the East Asia Summit (EAS), the Post Ministerial Conference with India (PMC+1), the ASEAN Regional Forum (ARF), the ASEAN Defence Ministers' Meeting (ADMM) Plus, and other ASEAN-India ministerial/sectoral mechanisms.

4. Continue to support and contribute to ASEAN integration and ASEAN Community building process, towards

the realisation of the ASEAN Community Vision 2025.

Political and Security Cooperation:

5. Reaffirm our commitment to work closely together on common regional and international security issues of mutual concern and ensure an open, transparent, inclusive and rules-based regional architecture through existing ASEAN-led frameworks and mechanisms such as the PMC+1 with India, ARF, EAS, the ADMM-Plus, and ASEAN Senior Officials' Meeting on Transnational Crimes (SOMTC)+India Consultations.

6. Reaffirm the importance of maintaining and promoting peace, stability, maritime safety and security, freedom of navigation and overflight in the region, and other lawful uses of the seas and unimpeded lawful maritime commerce and to promote peaceful resolutions of disputes, in accordance with universally recognised principles of international law, including the 1982 United Nations Convention on the Law of the Sea (UNCLOS), and the relevant standards and recommended practices by the International Civil Aviation Organization (ICAO) and the International Maritime Organization (IMO). In this regard, we support the full and effective implementation of the Declaration on the Conduct of the Parties in the South China Sea (DOC) and look forward to an early conclusion of the Code of Conduct in the South China Sea (COC).

7. Strengthen maritime cooperation through existing relevant mechanisms including the Expanded ASEAN Maritime Forum (EAMF) to address common challenges on maritime issues.

8. Work together to prevent and manage accidents and incidents at sea and promote effective coordination between ASEAN and India in maritime search and rescue, in accordance with existing processes and practices, including those of the ICAO and IMO, as well as encourage increased engagement between research institutions on maritime issues and collaboration on maritime education, research,

development and innovation.

9. Deepen cooperation in combating terrorism in all its forms and manifestations, violent extremism and radicalisation through information sharing, law enforcement cooperation and capacity building under the existing ASEAN-led mechanisms such as ASEAN SOMTC+India Consultation and the ADMM-Plus Experts' Working Group on Counter-Terrorism (EWG CT) and frameworks such as the 2003 ASEAN-India Joint Declaration for Cooperation to Combat International Terrorism, the EAS Statement on Countering Violent Extremism in 2015, and the EAS Statement on Countering Ideological Challenges of Terrorism and Terrorist Narratives and Propaganda, and the EAS Leaders' Declaration on Anti-Money Laundering and Countering the Finance of Terrorism adopted in 2017, and the ARF Work Plan on Counter-Terrorism and Transnational Crime. In addition, strengthen cooperation and collaboration to combating other transnational crimes, including people smuggling, trafficking in persons, illicit drug trafficking, cyber crime, and piracy and armed robbery against ships.

10. Support the implementation of the Langkawi Declaration on the Global Movement of Moderates to promote peace, security, upholding rule of law, sustainable and inclusive development, equitable growth and social harmony.

11. Reiterate commitment and promote comprehensive approach to combat terrorism through close cooperation by disrupting and countering terrorists, terrorist groups and networks, including by countering cross-border movement of terrorists and foreign terrorist fighters and misuse of internet including social media by terror entities; strengthen cooperation to stop terrorism financing efforts, and prevent recruitment of members of terrorist groups; support efforts in targeting terrorist groups and sanctuaries; and take further urgent measures to counter and prevent the spread of terrorism, while stressing that there can be no justification for acts of terror on any grounds whatsoever.

12. Work together with the international community to

ensure compliance with the relevant United Nations Security Council resolutions regarding counter-terrorism, and to note efforts on the negotiations of the Comprehensive Convention on International Terrorism (CCIT) at the United Nations.

13. Strengthen cooperation between ASEAN and India on cyber-security capacity building and policy coordination, including through supporting the implementation of the ASEAN Cyber security Cooperation Strategy, ARF Work Plan on Security of and in the Use of Information and Communication Technologies (ICTs) and the work of ARF Inter-Sessional Meeting on Security of and in the use of ICTs and further strengthen regional cyber capacity building initiatives undertaken by the other ASEAN sectoral bodies and build on the discussions at the 2015 ASEAN-India Cyber Security Conference at the proposed First ASEAN-India Cyber Dialogue in 2018.

Economic Cooperation:

14. Further strengthen ASEAN-India economic relations, including through the full utilisation and effective implementation of the ASEAN-India Free Trade Area, and intensify efforts in 2018 toward the swift conclusion of a modern, comprehensive, high quality, and mutually beneficial Regional Comprehensive Economic Partnership (RCEP).

15. Cooperate for conservation and sustainable use of marine resources in the Indian and Pacific Oceans in accordance with international law, notably the United Nations Convention on the Law of the Sea (UNCLOS) and address threats to these resources including illegal, unreported and unregulated fishing, loss of coastal ecosystems and the adverse impacts of pollution, ocean acidification, marine debris, and invasive species on the marine environment. In this regard, explore cooperation in the field of blue economy, and take note of India's proposal for a possible framework of cooperation in this regard.

16. Deepen cooperation in the area of aviation under the ASEAN-India Aviation Cooperation Framework adopted at

the 14th ASEAN Transport Ministers' Meeting in Manila, on November 6, 2008, including through the convening of air services consultations by the ASEAN-India Working Group on Regional Air Services Arrangements and the establishment of air transport cooperation on technical, economic, and regulatory matters between ASEAN and India. Establish closer ASEAN-India air links to promote tourism, trade, and enhance greater connectivity between ASEAN and India.

17. Promote maritime transport cooperation between ASEAN and India, and encourage potential private sector participation in the development of seaports, maritime logistics network and maritime services in order to create greater efficient linkages; and encourage ASEAN and India to continue discussions on these priority areas.

18. Strengthen cooperation in the area of aviation and maritime transport and look forward to the expeditious conclusion of the ASEAN-India Air Transport Agreement (AI-ATA) and the ASEAN-India Maritime Transport Agreement (AI-MTA).

19. Strengthen cooperation in ICT to enhance ICT policies, build capacity, improve digital connectivity, infrastructure and services, develop ICT human resources through the establishment of Centres of Excellence in Software Development and Training (CESDT) in some ASEAN Member States, encourage ICT start-ups, and explore emerging technologies for adoption; in synergy with the Master Plan on ASEAN Connectivity 2025 and the ASEAN ICT Master Plan 2020, respectively.

20. Further promote stable and sustainable growth for micro, small and medium enterprises (MSMEs), including through technology transfer, diffusion, adoption and adaptation as well as enhancing capacity building, technical assistance, distribution channels, financing facilities, access to innovation, and opportunities to integrate into the global and regional value chains, as well as utilisation of Project Development Fund and Quick Impact Project Fund, where relevant.

21. Continue to enhance cooperation for ensuring long-term food and energy security in our region through strengthening cooperation in agriculture and energy sectors; work together to promote the development of renewable energy technology through international platforms including the International Solar Alliance (ISA) where applicable.

22. Continue to deepen sectoral relations in science and technology (S&T) through cooperation on the ASEAN-India Innovation Platform, ASEAN-India Research and Training Fellowship Scheme, and ASEAN-India Collaborative Research and Development Programme, in areas aligned with ASEAN Plan of Action on Science, Technology and Innovation (APASTI) 2016-2025, including, among others, nano technology, materials science and biotechnology; and enhance capacity building on S&T.

23. Continue to collaborate in peaceful exploitation of outer space, through the implementation of the ASEAN-India Space Cooperation Programme, including launching of satellites, their monitoring through telemetry tracking and command stations and usage of satellite image data for sustainable exploitation of ground, sea, atmospheric and digital resources for equitable development of the region, as well as explore cooperation in R&D in emerging space technologies such as small satellites, inter-satellite communications, satellite propulsion, and analytics for space data.

24. Continue to promote private sector engagement and strengthen business-to-business relations, including through the ASEAN-India Business Council, and encourage trade events to promote brand awareness of ASEAN and India products and services to further broaden and deepen economic linkages. We also look forward to the establishment of the ASEAN-India Trade and Investment Centre.

Socio-Cultural Cooperation:

25. Cooperate on the promotion of the civilisational and historical links between ASEAN and India by providing platforms for knowledge exchanges among policy makers,

managers, and the academicians concerned with tangible and intangible cultural heritage; intensify efforts to preserve, protect and restore cultural and historical symbols and structures which are of mutual interest in reflecting the ASEAN-India cultural and historical connection, including through India's proposal on mapping inscriptions along the Mekong river and organising of conferences and activities on ASEAN-India Cultural and Civilisational Links.

26. Encourage health cooperation in areas relevant to the ASEAN Post-2015 Health Development Agenda, particularly in the area of strengthening health system and access to care, as well as safe and good quality medical products and affordable quality medicines, including traditional and complementary medicines.

27. Cement a stronger cultural link by promoting cultural tourism and further enhancing people-to-people contacts, through programmes such as Delhi Dialogue, ASEAN-India Network of Think Tanks (AINTT), ASEAN-India Eminent Persons Lecture Series (AIEPLS), diplomats training courses, as well as exchange programmes for students, parliamentarians, farmers, media, and other youth programmes.

28. Strengthen cooperation in education and youth sectors, in the form of setting up of English Language Training, Entrepreneurship Development and Vocational Training Centres, and granting of annual scholarships; such as Indian Technical and Economic Cooperation (ITEC) scholarships, ASEAN-India Goodwill Scholarship, Nalanda scholarship, and explore the possibility of setting up an ASEAN-India network of universities, and encourage other University to University exchanges, including with ASEAN University Network.

29. Strengthen ASEAN-India cooperation in disaster management and humanitarian assistance, including supporting the work of the ASEAN Coordinating Centre for Humanitarian Assistance on disaster management (AHA Centre) in the realisation of the ASEAN Declaration on One ASEAN, One Response: ASEAN Responding to Disaster as

One in The Region and Outside The Region and establishing close partnership between the AHA Centre and its Indian counterpart for better coordination in regional disaster management.

30. Promote dialogue between government officials and relevant stakeholders of ASEAN and India on empowerment of women, the promotion and protection of the rights of women and children, the elimination of all forms of violence against them, and promotion of women entrepreneurs in line with the ASEAN-India Plan of Action (POA) 2016-2020, as well as support relevant ASEAN frameworks and mechanisms on these matters.

31. Promote cooperation in environmental management and climate change, including exploring cooperation to support the implementation of relevant strategic measures as outlined in the ASCC Blueprint 2025, priorities of the ASEAN Senior Officials on Environment (ASOEN), and the ASEAN Working Group on Climate Change (AWGCC) Work Plan 2016-2025.

32. Enhance cooperation in biodiversity conservation and management, through exchange of knowledge and experience, conduct of joint research activities and capacity building programmes to address the loss of biodiversity and ecosystem degradation, including supporting the work of the ASEAN Centre for Biodiversity (ACB).

33. Explore the possibility of cooperation in alliance building, networking and partnership between ASEAN and India in civil service matters, among others, training the civil servants of ASEAN countries for the purpose of supporting further integration of ASEAN community and implementation of the ASEAN Community Vision 2025.

Connectivity:

34. Reaffirm our commitment to enhance physical and digital connectivity in line with the MPAC 2025 and the AIM 2020 by, among others, availing of the US$1 billion line of credit announced by India to promote physical infrastructure and digital connectivity.

35. Encourage the early completion of the India-Myanmar-Thailand Trilateral Highway Project and extend this Trilateral Highway to Cambodia, Lao PDR and Vietnam.

Cooperation on Narrowing the Development Gap:

36. Welcome and appreciate India's continued support for ASEAN's efforts in narrowing the development gap within and between ASEAN Member States by implementing the IAI Work Plan III.

Adopted in New Delhi, India, on the Twenty-Fifth Day of January Two Thousand and Eighteen.

5

Research Methodology for India-ASEAN Trade Analysis

The present study is predominately based on secondary data to understand the trade specialization and trade competitiveness of India with respect to ASEAN members. Time period for the study is from 2001 to 2015 in order to understand the transition in competitiveness and specialization in trade from 2001-09 before AIFTA and from 2010-15 after AIFTA. Commodity classification is based on Harmonized System (HS) Classification up to 6-digit level of coding for measuring the competitiveness. The study is broadly analyzed with the application of the suitable tools.

5.1 Lafay Index

Lafay index measures and analyzes the changing pattern of trade specialization. Lafay's (1992) measure of revealed comparative advantage (RCA) is advancement over the Balassa index as it also includes imports as well. Lafay index defines a country's trade specialization with regards to a specific good as the difference between the trade balance of that good and the country's overall trade balance is weighed by the goods share in total trade.

Lafay index captures the intra-industry trade flows which have become a feature of the majority of industries. Another advantage of the Lafay's revealed comparative advantage index is that it is able to control distortion due to the macroeconomic fluctuations. Finally, Lafay index weighs each product's contribution according to its respective importance in trade.

$$LFI_j = 100\left(\frac{x_j - m_j}{x_j + m_j} - \frac{\sum_{j=1}^{N}(x_j - m_j)}{\sum_{j=1}^{N}(x_j + m_j)}\right)\frac{x_j + m_j}{\sum_{j=1}^{N}(x_j + m_j)}$$

X_j = Export of product "j" towards the rest of world
M_j= Import of product "j" from the rest of world
N = Number of traded products

Positive value of the Lafay index indicates comparative advantage of a given item and the larger the value the higher the degree of specialization, with the sector making a bigger contribution to the trade balance. On the contrary, negative value implies reliance on imports.

Advantages of Lafay index are as under:

- Lafay index takes into consideration both the indicators— exports as well as imports in comparison to RCA, which relies only on exports.
- Lafay index weighs each product's contribution according to the respective importance in trade.
- Lafay index is able to control distortion due to the macroeconomic fluctuations.

Possible shortcomings of Lafay index is that it may take a value close to zero for a sector, in which a "nation" is both an importer and an exporter of equivalent amount of commodities, in different sub-segments of a sector.

5.2 Revealed Comparative Advantage (RCA) Index

The concept of comparative advantage has been used enormously in most of the research studies to discuss the comparative advantage or competitiveness of a commodity. The first study in the area of RCA was made by Leisner (1958) by applying the simple model. The model was not a direct technique that could measure the comparative or competitive nature of a commodity. Later, a comprehensive and advanced measure of RCA was developed by Hungarian economist Bella Balassa (1965), also known as the Balassa index.

This model helps in measuring the comparative advantage

of a commodity and tells about the competing capability of the commodity in the market. The Balassa index does not aim to measure the comparative advantage of the countries in the near future, because RCA indices are established on the basis of actual data. Rather, the estimates derived over time using the RCA, indicate in which direction is the pattern of comparative advantage heading (Tamberi and Benedictis, 2001). The RCA index (RCAI), is used to compare the ratio of the share of industry (or product) in a country's total export, to the ratio of the share of industry (or product) in world's total export.

The formula for RCA index is given below:

$(RCA^i)_a = (X^i_a / X^i_t) \quad (X^w_a / X^w_t)$

Where: $(RCA^i)_a$= revealed comparative advantage of a country in a particular good.

X^i_a = Value of export of commodity *a* in country *i*

X^i_t= Value of total exports by country *i*

X^w_a= Value of world exports of commodity *a*

X^w_t= Value of total world exports

The values of the RCA index, shows the comparative advantage or the greater degree of specialization in the export of commodity *a*, if the $(RCA^i)_a$ value is greater than 1 and vice-versa (Mahmood, 2004).

The revealed comparative advantage application measured for the investigation is based on the mean difference of time periods of 2001-09 and 2010-15. The mean difference is only made because RCA is a steady technique and on mean terms it could at least give appropriate results regarding the comparative advantage of the commodities, as commodity comparative advantage changes with time but RCA technique due to its steadiness in nature may not provide better results. Thus, mean time of 2001-09 and 2010-15 period is taken for the comparative advantage of the commodities for the study period.

The RCA indices can also be useful in indicating that some of the products may possess a comparative disadvantage but might have a potential to achieve export competitiveness over a period of time. For this to be achieved, a country's exports are categorized into competitively positioned, emerging product (Tier-I and Tier-II), threatened product line and weakly positioned products (Tier-I and Tier-II).

5.2.1 Competitively Positioned Product Lines: These product lines had RCA index greater than 1 and show reliable improvement over time due to constructive external as well as internal conditions. In this category fall the products that show:

- RCA index is greater than 1 during the average time period of 2010-15, i.e., $RCA_{2010-15} > 1$ for any product line.
- And also, difference between RCA index of any product line in average (time frame) for years 2010-15 and average of years 2001-09 is positive or greater than zero, i.e., $RCA_{2010-15} - RCA_{2001-09} > 0$

5.2.2 Threatened Products Lines: These product lines have RCAs greater than unity, but the indices are declining over time due to an adverse domestic environment and/or global competitive pressures. The decision principle to select products under this group is as follows:

- $RCA_{2010-15} > 1$ for a particular product line.
- Difference between average RCA of product line 2010-15 and RCA of product line 2001-09 is negative, i.e., $RCA_{2010-15} - RCA_{2001-09} < 0$.

5.2.3 Emerging Product: This product lines demonstrates and states the RCA indices that are less than 1, which reflects the revealed comparative disadvantage in the product, but their relative global position in the exports market is doing better. These products have been further sub-categorized into two more options which are:

Tier-I: It contains those product lines where:

$RCA_{2010-15} <$ but equals to 0.5 or > 0.5 during the average period of 2010-15.

Difference between the RCA averages of 2012-13 and 2001-05 is positive for the concerned product lines, i.e.,

$RCA_{2010-15} - RCA_{2001-09} > 0$

Tier-II: It contains those product lines where:

$RCA_{2010-15} < 0.5$

Difference between the RCA averages of 2010-15 and 2001-09 is positive for the concerned product line, i.e.,

$RCA_{2010-15} - RCA_{2001-09} > 0$

5.2.4 Weakly Positioned Product: RCA indices of these product lines are less than unity and declining due to non-advantageous global and domestic factors. This product line is further sub-divided into following sections.

Tier-I: It contains those product lines that exhibit:

$RCA_{2010-15} < 1$ but equal to 0.5 or > 0.5 in the same period.

Difference between the RCA averages of 2010-15 and 2001-09 is negative for the concerned product line, i.e.,

$RCA_{2010-15} - RCA_{2001-09} < 0$

Tier-II: In this group are product lines that show:

$RCA_{2010-15} < 0.5$

Difference between the RCA averages of 2010-15 and 2001-09 is negative for the concerned product line, i.e.,

$RCA_{2010-15} - RCA_{2001-09} < 0$

5.3 Revealed Import Dependence (RID) Index

The concept of import dependence has been used largely in most of the research studies to discuss the comparative disadvantage and to identify the commodities, which have more import dependence for the partner countries. As revealed comparative advantage (RCA) represents competitiveness and comparative advantage, the revealed import dependence index (RID) shows high dependency and comparative disadvantage of a particular nation in a particular product category.

This index helps in assessing the comparative disadvantage of the commodity and tells about the falling competing capability of the commodity in the market. The RID index does not aim to calculate the comparative disadvantage of the nation in the near future, because RID indices are based upon the actual data. Rather, the estimates derived over time using the RID, indicate in which direction the pattern of comparative disadvantage is heading (Wani et al., 2014). The RID index is defined as the ratio of the commodity's share in country's total imports, to the ratio of its share in total world imports.

The formula for RID Index is given as follows:

$(RID^i)_a = (M^i_a / M^i_t) \quad (M^w_a / M^w_t)$

Where:

$(RID^i)_a$= Revealed import dependence of country in a particular good.

M^i_a = Value of import of commodity *a* in country *i*

M^i_t= Value of total imports by country *i*

M^w_a= Value of world imports of commodity *a*

M^w_t= Value of total world imports

The values of the RID index exceeding unity suggest a strong dependence of the nation on the import of a specific item in a reference period and vice-versa.

The Revealed import dependence index measured for the analysis is based upon the mean difference of time periods from 2001-09 and 2010-15. The mean difference is only made because RID is a steady technique and on mean terms it could give at least the appropriate results regarding the dependency of the commodities, as a commodity's comparative disadvantage changes with time but RID technique being static in nature may not provide better results. Thus, the mean time of 2001-09 and 2010-15 period is taken for the study period.

The RID indices can also be useful to demonstrate that some of the products may possess a comparative disadvantage or high import dependency at present but might possess a potential to achieve comparative advantage over a period of time. For this to be achieved, a country's imports are categorized into rising dependence, emerging threatened product (Tier-I and Tier-II), less threatened product (Tier-I and Tier-II) and rising independence.

5.3.1 Rising Dependence Product: These product lines had RID index greater than unity and display a rising dependence for that particular product line, thereby inferring a comparative disadvantage in the product line. In this category, products show as follows:

- RID index is greater than 1 during the average time period of 2010-15, i.e., $RID_{2010\text{-}15} > 1$ for any product line.
- And also, difference between RID index of any product line in average (time frame) of years 2010-15 and average of years 2001-09 is positive, i.e.

  $RCA_{2010\text{-}15} - RCA_{2001\text{-}09} > 0$

5.3.2 Emerging Threatened Products: These product lines indicate RID value to be greater than zero, and the indices difference is turning out to be positive thereby revealing a comparative disadvantage in the product line. This product line has been categorized into two more headings:

Tier-I: It contains those product lines where:

$RCA_{2010\text{-}15} < 1$ but equals to 0.5 or >0.5 for the average period of 2010-15.

Difference between the RID averages of 2012-13 and 2001-05 is positive for the concerned product lines, i.e.,

$RCA_{2010\text{-}15} - RCA_{2001\text{-}09} > 0$

Tier-II: It contains those product lines where:

$RCA_{2010\text{-}15} < 0.5$

Difference between the RID averages of 2010-15 and 2001-09 is positive for the concerned product line, i.e.,

$RID_{2010\text{-}15} - RID_{2001\text{-}09} > 0$

5.3.3 Less Threatened Product: These product lines indicate RID value to less than zero, and indices difference turn out to be negative, thereby revealing a comparative advantage or lack of import dependency for the particular product line. This product line has been categorized into two more sections:

Tier-I: It contains those product lines that exhibit:

$RID_{2010\text{-}15} < 1$ but equal to 0.5 or > 0.5 in the same period.

Difference between the RID averages of 2010-15 and 2001-09 is negative for the concerned product line, i.e.,

$RID_{2010\text{-}15} - RID_{2001\text{-}09} < 0$

Tier-II: In this group are product lines that show:

$RID_{2010\text{-}15} < 0.5$

Difference between the RID averages of 2010-15 and

2001-09 is negative for the concerned product line, i.e.,

$RID_{2010-15} - RID_{2001-09} < 0$

5.3.4 Rising Independence Product: These product lines had RID index greater than one and the negative value of the index difference infers rising independence for that particular product line, thereby inferring a comparative advantage in the product line.

In this category, the products show as under:

- $RID_{2010-15} > 1$.
- Difference between the RID averages of 2010-15 and 2001 09 is negative for the concerned product line, i.e.,

  $RID_{2010-15} - RID_{2001-09} < 0$

5.4 Operational Definition of Industry Level

There are various ways to categorize the industry at various levels. However, the present study describes the definition of the industry level that has been categorized into six different sub-categories as proposed by Basu and Das (2011).

1. Non-fuel primary commodity;
2. Resource intensive manufactures;
3. Low skill and technology intensive manufactures;
4. Medium skill and technology intensive manufactures,
5. High skill and technology intensive manufactures and lastly;
6. Mineral fuel manufactures.

5.4.1 Non-fuel Primary Commodities: Non-fuel primary commodities are the output of the primary division of the economy such as raw materials and agricultural goods. The raw material has been illustrated with examples such as industrial metals, coal, oil, bauxite, copper and tin. It excludes precious metals such as gold. Similarly, the examples of agricultural goods are forestry and fishery output which constitutes of products such as wheat, beef, coffee, timber, fish and beverages. Another definition of non-fuel primary commodities include materials in natural or semi-finished state, such as ore, fresh fruits etc., which are extracted or harvested and need minimum processing before being used.

5.4.2 Resource Intensive Manufactures: Resource intensive manufactures are inclined to be simple and are typically labour-intensive in nature (for example, basic wood and woods products, tides and skin etc.) and still there exists a segment of products using skill-intensive technologies, capital and scale (such as textile and textile articles, footwear and headgears and article of stones, plaster, cement and mica). Therefore, the competitive advantage in these manufactures emerges usually but not always because of the availability of local natural resources and hence, do not raise significant issues for competitiveness.

5.4.3 Low Skill and Technology Intensive Manufactures: Low skill and technology intensive manufactures tend to possess well balanced and well diffused technologies. The high end technology is predominantly incorporated in the capital equipments and the low end of the manufacture range holds relatively simple skill requirements. Mostly traded manufactures under low skill and technology intensive are identical and compete on the ground of price and hence labour cost stands to be an essential element of cost in competitiveness. The economies to scale and barrier to entry are usually low. With income elasticity below one, the final markets grow slowly under low skill and technology.

Hence, it should be considered that manufactures of vital interest for the developing nations tends to be under lower skill technology segment, and are truly built upon low technologies and price rather than high quality competitiveness.

5.4.4 Medium Skill and Technology Intensive Manufactures: Medium skill and technology intensive manufactures comprehend the bulk of skill intensive technology in the intermediate and capital products are the central and most important part of industrial activity in fully developed economies. These manufactures tend to possess complex technology, with somewhat high level of research and development (R&D),

advanced skills and lengthy learning outcomes. The medium skill and technology intensive manufactures have been divided into two sub-groups at product level. MST (1): machinery and mechanical appliances are of export interest to newly industrializing countries. MST (2): automotive products (transportation equipments) have a stable and undifferentiated product line, generally with large scale facilities and technological effort in improving the equipment.

5.4.5 High Skill and Technology Intensive Manufactures: High skill and technology intensive manufactures possess the advanced and swiftly changing technologies, with high level of investment in research and development (R&D) and prominence on product designing. The highly advanced technologies need sophisticated infrastructure, high degree of specialized technical skill and lastly, close interaction amongst firms and research institutions. However, some products such as chemicals and electronics fall in a particular category.

Therefore, apart from chemicals and electronics, other high technology intensive manufactures (aircraft, measuring and musical instruments) remain entitled to countries or nations with high level of technology and skills. The comparative advantage of high skill and technology intensive manufactures continue to be dominated by general technological factors.

5.4.6 Mineral Fuel Commodity: Mineral fuel commodities are not the output of the primary division of the economy. For processing of mineral fuels for work of art, collector's pieces, measuring and musical instruments, pearls, precious or semi-precious stones etc. combination of both medium skill and high skill technology is required.

6

India-ASEAN Trade: Trends and Pattern

6.1 Introduction

International trading system has observed and registered the rapid increase of regional trade agreements (RTAs) in the 1990s, particularly in the post-WTO period. Indian economy has changed structurally since 1991 as the import-led growth strategy was restored by the export-led growth model. The opening up of Indian economy made it more export friendly and an environment that could lead to rapid growth and development. India started with the regional trade in order to expand the trade volume and encourage the economic cooperation among the regions. Indo-ASEAN economy is a dynamic and vibrant regional grouping in Asia.

After realizing the significance of the Asian region for substantial elevated trade growth, India announced it's "Look East" policy to strive for expanding its engagement and ties with East Asian nations. On October 8, 2003, India-ASEAN signed a Comprehensive Economic Cooperation Agreement (CECA) with a perspective to provide an institutional framework that allows economic cooperation to come into effect. Negotiation on Trade in Goods Agreement started in March 2004 and finally after six long years of negotiations, India-ASEAN Free Trade Agreement was signed on August 13, 2009 in Bangkok. The Agreement came into effect on January 1, 2010, which only enables trade in goods and commodities between India and ASEAN members.

6.2 India's Bilateral Trade with ASEAN:

ASEAN-India Free Trade Agreement (AIFTA) has fostered the acute and intense dialogue on the economic impact on India's trade in goods. ASEAN-India Free Trade Agreement (AIFTA) has stimulated and magnified the bilateral trade within the two economic regions. India-ASEAN trade relations has been exhibited and demonstrated in Table 6.1, using the data that represents the value of export, import, total trade and trade balance for the period 2001 to 2015.

Table 6.1: India's Bilateral Trade with ASEAN

(US$ billion)

Year	Export	Import	Total Trade	Trade Balance
2001	03.31	04.34	07.66	-01.03
2002	04.50	04.80	09.31	-00.30
2003	05.07	06.68	11.75	-01.61
2004	07.55	08.55	16.10	-00.99
2005	10.28	10.63	20.91	-00.34
2006	12.36	16.30	28.67	-03.93
2007	13.82	21.03	34.85	-07.20
2008	19.43	26.69	46.13	-07.26
2009	17.89	23.96	41.86	-06.06
2010	22.95	29.64	52.59	-06.68
2011	34.49	40.33	74.82	-05.83
2012	32.29	42.73	75.03	-10.44
2013	37.88	42.30	80.19	-04.42
2014	31.29	44.45	75.75	-13.16
2015	26.42	41.51	67.94	-15.08

Sources: Calculated from UNCTAD*Stat;* Ministry of Commerce and Industry, Government of India.

Table 6.2 exhibits the trends and pattern of India's export growth in ASEAN region with respect of India's global/total export growth over the years. The data provided gives an insight that export growth in ASEAN region is more than that of India's global export growth. From 35.84 in year 2002 to 50.26 in 2011, the export growth rate in ASEAN region was higher in comparison with global export growth which was pegged at 14.17 in year 2002 and rose to 36.78 during the year 2011.

Similarly, India's export share also depicts the same trend and pattern. The export share was minimal with 7.55 percent share in year 2001 and jumped to 11.44 percent in year 2011. But exports' growth to ASEAN region has witnessed a downward trend within two consecutive years, viz., -05.66 in year 2014 and -16.74 in 2015.

Table 6.2: India's Exports to ASEAN: 2001-2015

(US$ billion)

Year	Export to ASEAN	India's Global Export	India's Export Growth in ASEAN	India's Global Export Growth	Export Share (%)
2001	3.31	43.87	-	-	07.55
2002	4.51	50.09	35.84	14.17	08.98
2003	5.07	59.36	12.62	18.48	08.94
2004	7.55	75.91	48.92	27.86	09.95
2005	10.28	100.35	36.11	32.20	10.24
2006	12.36	121.21	20.25	20.77	10.21
2007	13.82	145.89	11.76	20.37	09.47
2008	19.43	181.86	40.57	24.64	10.68
2009	17.89	176.76	-07.89	-02.82	10.12
2010	22.95	220.48	28.26	24.69	10.41
2011	34.49	301.48	50.26	36.78	10.44
2012	32.29	289.56	-06.38	-03.95	11.15
2013	37.88	336.61	17.31	16.24	11.25
2014	31.29	317.54	-17.55	-05.66	09.85
2015	26.42	264.38	-15.54	-16.74	09.99

Sources: Calculated from UNCTAD*Stat;* Ministry of Commerce and Industry, Government of India.

On the contrary to export growth, India's import growth from the ASEAN region has demonstrated and followed mixed trends during the study period from 10.62 in year 2002 to 23.66 in 2010 and finally at -06.61 in year 2015.

Interestingly, India's import percent share from ASEAN region has remained constant throughout, with an average of 8.92 percent for the period 2001 to 2015. The average of import growth from ASEAN region was registered at 18.86, which is higher in contrast to the average of global import growth at 17.46 for the years 2001 to 2015. The detailed analysis has been shown in Table 6.3.

Table 6.4 demonstrates that India's trade growth in ASEAN region has witnessed an asymmetrical and irregular trend in comparison with India's global trade growth. India's trade growth in ASEAN region varied from 21.53 in 2002 to -09.29 in 2009 to 0.27 in 2012 and to -10.31 in 2015, which gives a clear and unambiguous result on the trends and pattern of India-ASEAN trade.

Table 6.3: India's Import Growth in ASEAN: 2001 to 2015

(US$ billion)

Years	Imports from ASEAN	India's Global Imports	India's Import Growth in ASEAN	India's Global Import Growth	Import Share (%)
2001	4.34	50.67	-	-	08.57
2002	4.80	57.45	10.62	13.38	08.36
2003	6.68	72.43	39.09	26.06	09.23
2004	8.54	98.98	27.86	36.65	08.63
2005	10.63	140.86	24.35	42.31	07.54
2006	16.30	178.21	53.31	26.51	09.14
2007	21.03	218.64	29.01	22.68	09.61
2008	26.69	315.71	26.94	44.39	08.45
2009	23.96	266.40	-10.22	-15.61	08.99
2010	29.64	350.02	23.66	31.39	08.46
2011	40.33	462.40	36.07	32.11	08.72
2012	42.73	488.97	05.96	05.74	08.74
2013	42.30	466.04	-01.04	-04.68	09.07
2014	44.45	459.36	05.07	-01.43	09.67
2015	41.51	390.74	-06.61	-14.93	10.62

Sources: Calculated from UNCTAD*Stat;* Ministry of Commerce and Industry, Government of India.

Table 6.4: India's Trade Growth with ASEAN: 2001 to 2015

(US$ billion)

Years	Trade ASEAN	India's Global Trade	Trade Growth with ASEAN	India's Global Trade Growth	Trade Share (%)
2001	1.00	94.54	-	-	08.11
2002	9.31	107.55	21.53	13.75	08.65
2003	11.75	131.79	26.29	22.53	08.92
2004	16.10	174.88	36.94	32.69	09.21
2005	20.91	241.21	29.89	37.97	08.67

Contd...

2006	28.66	299.41	37.06	24.12	09.57
2007	34.85	364.54	21.57	21.75	09.56
2008	46.13	497.57	32.35	36.49	09.27
2009	41.86	443.16	-09.24	-10.93	09.44
2010	52.59	570.43	25.63	28.71	09.22
2011	74.82	763.88	42.26	33.91	09.79
2012	75.03	778.54	00.27	01.91	09.63
2013	80.19	802.65	06.87	03.09	10.01
2014	75.75	776.91	-05.53	-03.21	09.75
2015	67.94	655.12	-10.31	-15.67	10.37

Sources: Calculated from UNCTAD*Stat;* Ministry of Commerce and Industry, Government of India.

6.3 India-ASEAN Trade Analysis: Country-wise

Amongst the 10 member nations of the ASEAN region Singapore, Indonesia, Malaysia and Thailand are the dominant and main export destinations for the Indian exports. The ASEAN members like Cambodia, Brunei and Lao PDR are the least favourable trade destinations for India in the ASEAN region. Country-wise India's exports to the ASEAN region have been exhibited in Table 6.5.

Table 6.5: India's Export to ASEAN Countries: 2001 to 2015

(US$ billion)

Years	Brunei	Cambodia	Indonesia	Lao PDR	Malaysia
2001	0.0022	0.0105	0.4767	0.0057	0.7881
2002	0.0046	0.0169	0.7696	0.0021	0.7427
2003	0.0048	0.0202	1.0396	0.0005	0.7931
2004	0.0049	0.0167	1.2055	0.0009	1.0402
2005	0.0043	0.0213	1.3901	0.0065	1.1437
2006	0.0444	0.0481	1.8698	0.0023	1.3313
2007	0.0088	0.0448	1.8781	0.0029	1.8502
2008	0.0171	0.0538	2.6593	0.0045	3.0344
2009	0.0253	0.0415	3.0029	0.0269	3.5247
2010	0.0212	0.0611	4.5571	0.0081	3.5553
2011	0.8706	0.0895	6.4002	0.0139	3.7988
2012	0.0333	0.1101	6.0219	0.0273	3.7911
2013	0.0402	0.1367	5.5579	0.0613	5.4968
2014	0.0424	0.1541	4.4447	0.0636	4.6422
2015	0.0303	0.1453	2.8688	0.0512	4.8921

Contd...

Years	Myanmar	Philippines	Singapore	Thailand	Vietnam
2001	0.0576	0.2317	0.9261	0.5982	0.2179
2002	0.0739	0.4673	1.3803	0.7411	0.3044
2003	0.0766	0.3243	1.7019	0.7317	0.3788
2004	0.1126	0.3629	3.4164	0.8568	0.5348
2005	0.1172	0.4821	5.4255	1.0592	0.6334
2006	0.1241	0.5968	6.1272	1.3509	0.8741
2007	0.1627	0.5714	6.3901	1.6733	1.2414
2008	0.2373	0.7551	8.8539	2.0052	1.8126
2009	0.2081	0.6973	6.8275	1.7108	1.8335
2010	0.2725	0.8016	9.0662	2.1395	2.4755
2011	0.4558	1.0066	15.6244	2.7679	3.4665
2012	0.5268	1.1192	13.5527	3.4541	3.6581
2013	0.7428	1.4691	14.1891	4.2038	5.9876
2014	0.8685	1.4369	9.6766	3.4385	6.5265
2015	0.8599	1.3043	7.8051	3.1135	5.3572

Sources: Calculated from UNCTAD*Stat;* Ministry of Commerce and Industry, Government of India; and World Trade Organization.

Country-wise India's imports from ASEAN region are presented in Table 6.6.

Table 6.6: India's Import from ASEAN Countries: 2001 to 2015

(US$ billion)

Year	Brunei	Cambodia	Indonesia	Lao PDR	Malaysia
2001	0.0002	0.0011	0.9668	0.00	1.1523
2002	0.0003	0.0006	1.2632	0.00	1.3305
2003	0.0003	0.0003	1.8797	0.0002	1.8942
2004	0.0005	0.0002	2.4276	0.00	2.2144
2005	0.0008	0.0004	3.0189	0.00	2.4359
2006	0.2257	0.0014	3.6104	0.0003	4.6559
2007	0.2341	0.0012	4.8403	0.00	5.7255
2008	0.3258	0.0042	6.4313	0.0005	7.4613
2009	0.4891	0.0037	7.5996	0.0001	4.9902
2010	0.2071	0.0076	9.6953	0.0201	5.9959
2011	0.7049	0.0084	13.9646	0.0701	9.1062
2012	0.9392	0.0101	14.0682	0.1437	10.4941
2013	0.7661	0.0127	14.9841	0.1113	9.3307
2014	0.9426	0.0164	15.1848	0.0596	10.9285
2015	0.6077	0.0429	13.9021	0.1429	9.5599

Contd...

Year	Myanmar	Philippines	Singapore	Thailand	Vietnam
2001	0.3504	0.0777	1.3547	0.4245	0.0173
2002	0.3528	0.1327	1.3336	3651	0.0281
2003	0.3502	0.1119	1.8671	0.5392	0.0335
2004	0.4106	0.1808	2.4921	0.7501	0.0732
2005	0.4891	0.2031	3.1594	1.1965	0.1273
2006	0.7026	0.2087	5.1845	1.5508	0.1598
2007	0.8091	0.1735	6.9016	2.1923	0.1531
2008	0.9062	0.2276	8.3047	2.6647	0.3716
2009	1.1818	0.3429	6.1416	2.7758	0.4429
2010	1.1221	0.3944	7.231	3.9408	0.9935
2011	1.2621	0.4502	8.1553	5.0555	1.5542
2012	1.3461	0.4941	7.7973	5.4992	1.9454
2013	1.3662	0.4087	7.0266	5.4754	2.8266
2014	1.3927	0.4006	7.0694	5.6809	2.7816
2015	1.0163	0.5181	7.3959	5.6501	2.6801

Sources: Calculated from UNCTAD*Stat;* Ministry of Commerce and Industry, Government of India; and World Trade Organization.

4.4 Commodity-wise India-ASEAN Trade Analysis

India's chief exporting commodities to the ASEAN region includes mineral fuel, mineral oils and products (HS code-27), meat and edible offal (HS code-02), nuclear reactor, boilers, machinery and mechanical appliances (HS code-84), organic chemicals (HS code-29), natural or cultured pearls, precious and semi-precious stones (HS code-71), fish and crustaceans, molluscs and other aquatic invertebrates (HS code-3).

India's top 25 exporting commodities to ASEAN region for the year 2015 are presented in Table 6.7.

Table 6.7: India's Top 25 Commodities Exported to ASEAN Region in 2015

S. No.	HS Code	Commodity	Export in 2015 (US$ mn.)	Share %
1.	27	Mineral fuels, mineral oils and products	3,863.48	14.61
2.	2	Meat and edible meat offal.	2,649.14	10.02
3.	84	Nuclear reactors, boilers, machinery and mechanical appliances	1,590.93	06.01
4.	29	Organic chemicals	1233.92	04.66

Contd...

5.	71	Natural or cultured pearls, precious or semiprecious stones	1091.99	04.13
6.	3	Fish and crustaceans, molluscs	1088.95	04.12
7.	87	Vehicles other than railway or tramway rolling stock	1051.43	03.97
8.	99	Miscellaneous goods	1040.20	03.93
9.	89	Ships, boats and floating structures	977.42	03.69
10.	85	Electrical machinery and equipment and parts thereof	795.78	03.01
11.	30	Pharmaceutical products	717.31	02.71
12.	12	Oil seeds and olea. fruits; misc. grains, seeds and fruit	607.33	02.29
13.	52	Cotton.	601.62	02.27
14.	17	Sugars and sugar confectionery	512.05	01.93
15.	9	Coffee, tea, mate and spices	510.62	01.89
16.	74	Copper and articles thereof	435.02	01.64
17.	72	Iron and steel	423.92	01.59
18.	90	Optical, photographic cinematographic measuring	356.33	01.34
19.	39	Plastic and articles thereof	347.72	01.31
20.	38	Miscellaneous chemical product	334.21	01.26
21.	76	Aluminium and articles thereof	322.41	01.21
22.	32	Tanning or dyeing extracts; tannins and their deri. dyes.	309.66	01.17
23.	75	Nickel and articles thereof	285.36	01.07
24.	73	Articles of iron or steel	267.05	01.01
25.	40	Rubber and articles thereof	225.93	00.85
Sum of Top 25 Commodities			21639.72	81.69
India's Total Export to ASEAN			26428.12	100.00

Source: Export-Import Data Bank, Ministry of Commerce and Industry, Government of India.

Major imports from the ASEAN countries include mineral fuel, mineral oils and products (HS code-27), animal or vegetable fats and oil and cleavage products (HS code-15), electrical machinery and equipments and parts thereof (HS code-85), nuclear reactors, boilers, machinery and mechanical appliances (HS code-84), organic chemicals (HS code-29), and plastics and articles thereof (HS code-39).

India's top 25 importing commodities from the ASEAN region for year 2015 are presented in Table 6.8.

Table 6.8: India's Top 25 Commodities Imported from ASEAN Region in 2015

S. No.	HS Code	Commodity	Import in 2015 (US$ mn)	Share %
1.	27	Mineral fuels, mineral oils and products	8033.42	19.35
2.	15	Animal or vegetable fats and oils and their cleavage product	5980.23	14.41
3.	85	Electrical machinery and equipment and parts thereof	4141.63	09.97
4.	84	Nuclear reactors, boilers, machinery and mechanical appliances	3741.05	09.01
5.	29	Organic chemicals	2074.60	04.99
6.	39	Plastic and articles thereof	1758.55	04.23
7.	89	Ships, boats and floating structures.	1099.75	02.64
8.	40	Rubber and articles thereof.	995.10	02.39
9.	44	Wood and articles of wood; wood charcoal	972.72	02.34
10.	72	Iron and steel	902.33	02.17
11.	07	Edible vegetables and certain roots	836.13	02.01
12.	26	Ores, slag and ash.	822.66	01.98
13.	71	Natural or cultured pearls, precious or semiprecious stones	816.83	01.97
14.	74	Copper and articles thereof	670.48	01.61
15.	38	Miscellaneous chemical products.	648.51	01.56
16.	90	Optical, photographic cinematographic measuring, checking precision	617.00	01.48
17.	87	Vehicles other than railway or tramway rolling stock	598.27	01.44
18.	73	Articles of iron or steel	369.38	00.88
19.	76	Aluminium and articles thereof	369.27	00.88
20.	28	Inorganic chemicals; organic or inorganic compounds of precious metals	329.12	00.79
21.	09	Coffee, tea, mate and spices.	287.81	00.69
22.	75	Nickel and articles thereof	273.61	00.65
23.	88	Aircraft, spacecraft, and parts	208.61	00.51
24.	48	Paper and paperboard; articles of paper pulp, of paper or of paperboard	206.55	00.49
25.	32	Tanning or dyeing extracts; tannins and their derivatives, dyes, pigments	190.28	00.45
Sum of Top 25 Commodities			36943.89	88.89
India's Total Imports from ASEAN			41516.39	100.00

Source: Export-Import Data Bank, Ministry of Commerce and Industry, Government of India.

7

Analysis of Trade Specialization

7.1 Introduction

The process of globalization which started in the early 1980s has observed a tremendous increase in the volume of international trade and the process of regional economic integration. Under the process of globalization, less developed countries (LDCs) have played a vital role in the diversification and enlargement of the world trade.

Indeed, the opening up of the economy for trade has been regarded as one of the essential and key aspect of the growth strategy. Hence, trade among different countries could be traditionally explained as emergence from the specialization of a country in specific product/industry as constrained by the country's relative factor endowments. Therefore, the gradual development of the trade specialization over a span of time is a phenomenon that generally reflects the deep structural change in entire economic structure of a nation.

According to Worz (2005), specialization could be explained as a technique where a business area and economy focuses on the production of goods and services to achieve a higher degree of productive efficiency. Hence, nations specialize by utilizing their comparative advantage arising from differences in factor endowments, technology and innovation. Therefore, in the light of rising awareness about the significance of specialization, it would be fascinating to undertake trade specialization from Indo-ASEAN context.

The objective to be analyzed in this chapter is to measure trade specialization of India with respect to ASEAN members using the Lafay index (LFI) on harmonized standard (HS) 6 digit level commodity classification, under six different levels of industries as proposed by Basu and Das (2011) viz.: (a) non-fuel primary commodities, (b) resource intensive; (c) low skill and technology intensive manufactures; (d) medium skill and technology intensive manufactures; (e) high skill and technology intensive manufactures; and (f) mineral fuels.

Lafay index (LFI) does not only consider exports and imports, but also the size of intra-industry trade. While considering the data span for the period 2001-2015, 2-year average value of Lafay index for 2001-02, 2004-05, 2009-10 and 2014-15 has been used. The 2-year average value of LFI has been selected to concentrate on these time periods because 2001-02 and 2014-15 are the beginning and the end of the time span in our study and 2004-05 is the time period in which Trade Negotiations in Goods Agreement started. Lastly, 2009-10 is the critical period because after six years of negotiations, AIFTA was signed in August 2009 and the Agreement came into force on January 1, 2010.

7.2 Pattern of Trade Specialization at Industry Level

7.2.1. Non-fuel Primary Commodities: Table 7.1 shows some interesting changing pattern over a period of time in the average specialization index under non-fuel primary commodities. Over the period of study, nation such as Brunei clearly highlights its drive towards higher level of trade specialization with an increasing LFI value from 1.59 in 2001-02 to 3.05 in 2009-10 and lastly to 3.55 in 2014-15. Cambodia shows the improvement in trade specialization under non-fuel primary commodities with a constant decline in the negative average Lafay value from -1.82 in 2001-02 to -1.71 in 2009-10 and -1.21 in 2014-15.

7.2.2. Resource Intensive Manufactures: Under resource intensive manufactures, Table 7.2 clearly illustrates some interesting alterations in the average specialization index.

7.2.3. Low Skill and Technology Intensive Manufactures: Table 7.3 shows that Brunei holds a deteriorating low trade specialization under low skill and technology intensive manufactures with respective LFI value at -0.32 in 2001-02,

-1.51 in 2009-10 and -1.68 in 2014-15.

Table 7.1: Average Lafay Index for Non-fuel Primary Commodities (2001-2015)

Country	2001-02	2004-05	2009-10	2014-15
Brunei	1.59	3.24	3.05	3.55
Cambodia	-1.82	-1.79	-1.71	-1.21
India	-1.04	-0.67	-0.39	-0.52
Indonesia	0.71	0.27	1.22	0.81
Lao	1.56	2.16	4.24	3.69
Malaysia	-0.44	0.29	0.33	0.18
Myanmar	-	-	-	0.51
Philippines	-0.64	-0.67	-0.99	-0.65
Singapore	-0.34	-0.37	-0.57	-0.61
Thailand	-0.03	-0.19	-0.21	-0.23
Vietnam	1.65	1.15	0.62	0.03

Source: UNCOMTRADE; researcher's calculation.

Table 7.2: Average Lafay Index for Resource Intensive Manufactures (2001-2015)

Country	2001-02	2004-05	2009-10	2014-15
Brunei	-0.41	-0.14	-0.91	-1
Cambodia	4.11	3.85	1.35	2.66
India	1.21	0.87	0.58	0.64
Indonesia	1.05	0.74	0.43	0.41
Lao	1.62	1.53	0.11	0.09
Malaysia	0.11	0.13	0.10	0.09
Myanmar	-	-	-	0.91
Philippines	0.23	0.18	0.12	0.16
Singapore	-0.08	-0.06	-0.07	-0.09
Thailand	0.42	0.31	0.18	0.14
Vietnam	0.72	0.74	0.86	0.91

Source: UNCOMTRADE; researcher's calculation.

Further, Cambodia demonstrates an improvement in the average trade specialization index with decreasing negative LFI value from -2.25 in 2004-05 to -1.72 in 2009-10 and lastly to -1.07 in 2014-15. India exhibited an exponential rise in trade specialization for the time span of 2001-02 to 2014-15. India started achieving trade specialization with an increasing LFI value of 0.21 in 2001-02 to 0.25 in 2009-10 and finally to 0.28 for 2014-15, thereby revealing less of import dependency for India for low skill and technology intensive manufactures.

Table 7.3: Average Lafay Index for Low Skill and Technology Intensive Manufactures (2001-2015)

Country	2001-02	2004-05	2009-10	2014-15
Brunei	-0.32	-0.36	-1.51	-1.68
Cambodia	-1.03	-2.25	-1.72	-1.07
India	0.21	0.24	0.25	0.28
Indonesia	-0.54	-0.61	-0.63	-0.51
Lao	-0.41	-1.16	-1.22	-1.17
Malaysia	-0.59	-0.35	-0.34	-0.25
Myanmar	-	-	-	-0.61
Philippines	-0.32	-0.29	-0.21	-0.12
Singapore	-0.13	-0.12	-0.08	-0.11
Thailand	-0.47	-0.62	-0.54	-0.54
Vietnam	-1.16	-0.92	-0.91	-0.48

Source: UNCOMTRADE; researcher's calculation.

7.2.4. Medium Skill and Technology Intensive Manufactures: Under medium skill and intensive manufactures, Table 7.4 clearly exemplifies some interesting changing patterns over the time period 2001 to 2015. Brunei as one of the emerging nations of ASEAN clearly spotlights with continuous deterioration in its trade specialization index for medium skill and technology manufactures for the time span 2001-02 to 2014-15 with respective LFI values at -0.35 in 2001-02 to -0.65 in 2014-15.

7.2.5. High Skill and Technology Intensive Manufactures: From Table 7.5, it could be inferred that Brunei shows a mixed trend of trade specialization under the high skill and technology intensive manufactures. Brunei demonstrates a continuous decline in trade specialization for the high skill and technology intensive manufactures with a constant rise in LFI value from -0.29 in 2001-02 to -0.69 in 2009-10 and -0.91 in 2014-15. On the contrary, Cambodia exhibits an improvement in trade specialization under average trade specialization index. The negative LFI value for Cambodia, reduced constantly from -1.08 in 2004-05 to -0.68 in 2014-15, exhibiting a decreasing dependence on imports under the high skill and technology intensive manufactures.

Table 7.4: Average Lafay Index for Medium Skill and Technology Intensive Manufactures (2001-2015)

Country	2001-02	2004-05	2009-10	2014-15
Brunei	-0.35	-0.21	-0.57	-0.65
Cambodia	-2.31	-1.39	-0.88	-0.72
India	-0.11	-0.09	-0.06	0.12
Indonesia	-0.67	-0.76	-0.87	-0.74
Lao	-1.59	-1.68	-1.88	-2.21
Malaysia	-1.32	-0.52	-0.48	-0.35
Myanmar	-	-	-	-0.84
Philippines	-0.27	0.18	0.03	-0.01
Singapore	-0.34	-0.23	-0.09	-0.08
Thailand	-0.28	0.05	0.18	0.49
Vietnam	-1.06	-0.81	-0.71	-0.69

Source: UNCOMTRADE; researcher's calculation.

Table 7.5: Average Lafay Index for High Skill and Technology Intensive Manufactures (2001-2015)

Country	2001-02	2004-05	2009-10	2014-15
Brunei	-0.49	-0.34	-0.69	-0.91
Cambodia	-0.69	-1.08	-0.94	-0.68
India	-0.27	-0.23	-0.21	-0.18
Indonesia	0.1	-0.24	-0.61	-0.64
Lao	-1.31	-1.04	-0.91	-0.33
Malaysia	-1.67	0.11	0.52	0.81
Myanmar	-	-	-	-0.49
Philippines	0.58	0.32	0.11	0.43
Singapore	0.31	0.45	0.48	0.52
Thailand	-0.13	0.05	0.06	0.03
Vietnam	-0.77	-0.73	-0.71	-0.17

Source: UNCOMTRADE; researcher's calculation.

7.2.6 Mineral Fuel Manufactures: Under mineral fuel manufactures, Table 7.6 clearly exemplifies some of the interesting changing patterns over the time period from 2001 to

2015 in the average specialization index. Brunei as one of the emerging ASEAN member, clearly illustrates the negatively low and deteriorating trend in the trade specialization index.

Table 7.6: Average Lafay Index for Mineral Fuel Manufactures (2001-2015)

Country	2001-02	2004-05	2009-10	2014-15
Brunei	-0.64	-0.67	-0.68	-1.21
Cambodia	0.45	3.3	19.89	-1.19
India	-1.88	-1.43	0.21	0.23
Indonesia	0.41	0.23	0.31	0.77
Lao	-1.29	-0.91	-0.41	-0.93
Malaysia	-0.57	-0.61	-0.71	-0.12
Myanmar	-	-	-	-0.45
Philippines	0.06	0.02	-0.03	-0.04
Singapore	1.11	0.91	1.75	2.31
Thailand	0.81	-0.09	0.32	-0.31
Vietnam	-1.31	-1.28	-1.17	-0.04

Source: UNCOMTRADE; researcher's calculation.

The LFI value of Brunei for 2001-02 was -0.64, which further increased to -0.68 for 2009-10 and lastly to -1.21 for 2014-15. India, Indonesia and Singapore demonstrated a positive trend of increasing trade specialization under the average trade specialization index. The average Lafay index value for India was -1.43 in 2004-05, 0.21 in 2009-10 and lastly at 0.23 for the year 2014-15. The average Lafay index value of Indonesia and Singapore for the period 2001-15 is depicted in Table 7.6, revealing a low import dependence of both the nations under the mineral fuel intensive manufactures.

8

India-ASEAN Trade: Industry-wise Export Competitiveness

With the rise of globalization and the emergence of regional integration, both the processes have had a significant impact on the international trade system. Notably, the large part of the growth in world trade especially among developing nations is because of the simultaneous increase in export of the products that are close substitutes for each other in terms of factor inputs and consumption. The composition and volume of the trade both describe the export performance of a nation and the three major determinants of the global trade such as liberalization, technological advancements and rise in the national income furthermore depict the competitive position of a particular country in the international market (Mahmood, 2004).

8.1 Non-fuel Primary Commodities

Out of 9,741 HS 6 digit level product line, 1,456 (14.97 percent of the total) possess the RCA value to be greater than unity and the average RCA differences are still increasing, thereby placing them under "competitively positioned product" category. Table 8.1 clearly reveals that Myanmar portrays the highest percentage share at 27.69 in competitively positioned products followed by Philippines with a 23.82 percent share and Indonesia with a 15.65 percent share. The RCA profile of the "non-fuel primary products" highlights the lack of headway made by India with just a 14.7 percent share, positioning it just ahead of Cambodia, Singapore and Brunei. Therefore, it is important, that if the Indian economy has to gain more advantage of growing global trade, it should improve its production base for competitively positioned products such as 'vegetable products' (HS 05) and 'animal and animal products' (HS 01-05) to have a competitive edge.

Table 8.1: RCA Profile for Non-Fuel Primary Commodities (2001-2015)

Country	CP	TP	EP (I)	EP (II)	WP (I)	WP (II)	Total
Brunei	9 (2.2)	2 (0.4)	7 (1.7)	302 (74.3)	0 (0.0)	86 (21.1)	406 (4.1)
Cambodia	41 (14.0)	15 (5.1)	16 (5.4)	137 (46.9)	3 (1.0)	80 (27.3)	292 (2.9)
India	184 (14.7)	101 (8.2)	87 (6.9)	381 (30.5)	42 (3.3)	453 (36.2)	1248 (12.8)
Indonesia	173 (15.6)	80 (7.2)	29 (2.6)	334 (30.2)	29 (2.6)	460 (41.6)	1105 (11.3)
Lao	68 (18.1)	33 (8.8)	21 (5.6)	143 (38.1)	4 (1.0)	106 (28.2)	375 (3.8)
Malaysia	188 (15.0)	44 (3.5)	86 (6.8)	614 (49.1)	30 (2.4)	286 (22.9)	1248 (12.8)
Myanmar	190 (27.6)	0 (0)	34 (4.9)	462 (67.3)	0 (0.0)	0 (0.0)	686 (7.0)
Philippines	187 (23.8)	22 (2.8)	33 (4.2)	331 (42.1)	9 (1.1)	203 (25.8)	785 (8.0)
Singapore	61 (4.8)	38 (3.0)	41 (3.3)	552 (44.0)	27 (2.0)	533 (42.5)	1252 (12.8)
Thailand	186 (14.8)	91 (7.2)	64 (5.1)	493 (39.3)	40 (3.1)	379 (30.2)	1253 (12.8)
Vietnam	169 (15.4)	90 (8.0))	49 (4.4)	373 (34.1)	31 (2.8)	379 (34.7)	1091 (11.1)

Note: Numbers in parenthesis are percentage shares in the respective product line.

Notes: CP = Competitive Positioned Products; TP = Threatened Products; EP (I) = Emerging Products Tier-I; EP (II) Emerging Products Tier-II; WP (I) = Weakly Positioned Products Tier-I and WP (II) = Weakly Positioned Products Tier-II.

Source: UNCOMTRADE; calculations by the researcher.

Under emerging products (Tier-II), Brunei constitutes the highest percentage share of 74.38 followed by Myanmar and Malaysia with their respective percentage share of 67.34 and 49.19 percent. Therefore, the profile draws a special attention that nations such as Vietnam, India and Indonesia possess a low percent share in the emerging product Tier-II category with their respective percentage values to be at 34.18, 30.52 and 30.22 in comparison with other nations. Table 8.1 highlights that India should cautiously investigate for higher potentiality and competency in the world market thereby increasing its percentage share for emerging products Tier-II such as 'mineral products' (HS 25-75) and 'animal and vegetable fat oils (HS 15).

8.2 Resource Intensive Manufactures

Under resource intensive manufactures, out of a total of 9,791 HS 6 digit level product line, 1,410 of them (14.40 percent of the total) possess RCA value to be greater than 1 and the average RCA differences are still increasing, thereby placing them under "competitively positioned products" category.

Table 8.2 illustrates that Philippines stands highest with a 23.28 percent share in competitively positioned products followed by Vietnam with a 22.42 percent share and India placed at third position with a 21.41 percent share for 'textile and textile articles' (HS 50-63). The profile highlights that nations like Lao PDR, Thailand and Brunei constitute a low percent share for competitively positioned products which states the lack of competitive advantage, as is manifest in Table 8.2.

Weakly positioned products have been sub-divided into two categories viz. Tier-I and Tier-II. In the first category of Tier-I, there are a total of 422 product lines that depict a percentage of 4.31 of the total product line. Table 8.2 clearly explains that Thailand with a percent share of 9.68 is the highest in this product line followed by India with a percent share of 5.97 for 'textile and textile articles' (50-63) and Indonesia with a percent share of 5.37. Emerging nations such as Myanmar, Brunei and Cambodia possess a higher degree of comparative advantage in this product line with a low percentage share as is evident in Table 8.2.

India's large percent share in Tier-I category indicates a higher degree of comparative disadvantage in this resource intensive product grouping in comparison with other economies of the ASEAN members.

Table 8.2: RCA Profile for Resource Intensive Manufactures (2001-2015)

Country	CP	TP	EP (I)	EP (II)	WP (I)	WP (I)	Total
Brunei	7 (1.2)	2 (0.3)	6 (1.0)	318 (58.1)	2 (0.3)	212 (38.7)	547 (5.5)
Cambodia	33 (8.3)	5 (1.2)	17 (4.3)	236 (59.7)	2 (0.5)	102 (25.8)	395 (4.0)
India	269 (21.4)	228 (17.9)	66 (5.2)	242 (19.2)	75 (5.9)	376 (29.9)	1256 (12.8)
Indonesia	214 (17.6)	167 (13.8)	76 (6.2)	228 (18.8)	65 (5.3)	460 (38.0)	1210 (12.3)
Lao	46 (7.6)	42 (7.0)	22 (3.6)	209 (34.9)	23 (3.8)	256 (42.8)	598 (6.1)
Malaysia	131 (10.7)	45 (3.6)	75 (6.1)	394 (32.3)	39 (3.2)	534 (43.8)	1218 (12.4)
Myanmar	143 (19.5)	0 (0.0)	29 (3.9)	560 (76.5)	0 (0.0)	0 (0.0)	732 (7.4)
Philippines	228 (23.2)	60 (6.1)	30 (3.0)	288 (29.4)	26 (2.6)	347 (35.4)	979 (9.9)
Singapore	50 (8.6)	12 (2.0)	49 (8.5)	368 (63.8)	28 (4.8)	69 (11.9)	576 (5.8)
Thailand	23 (2.1)	139 (12.7)	80 (7.3)	241 (22.0)	106 (9.6)	505 (46.1)	1094 (11.1)
Vietnam	266 (22.4)	184 (15.5)	62 (5.2)	259 (21.8)	56 (4.7)	359 (30.2)	1186 (12.0)

Note: Numbers in parenthesis are percentage shares in the respective product line.

Notes: CP = Competitive Positioned Products; TP = Threatened Products; EP (I) = Emerging Products Tier-I; EP (II) Emerging Products Tier-II; WP (I) = Weakly Positioned Products Tier-I and WP (II) = Weakly Positioned Products Tier-II.

Source: UNCOMTRADE; calculations by the researcher.

8.3 Low Skill and Technology Intensive Manufacturing

Competitively positioned products possess an RCA value greater than unity. Table 8.3 encapsulates that Vietnam constitutes the highest percent share of 16.66 in competitively positioned products followed by India at the second position with a 15.84 percent share for 'base metal and articles' (HS 72-83) and both Malaysia and Philippines are positioned at third place with a 14.00 percent share in low skill and technology intensive manufactures.

The RCA profile of the "low skill and technology

intensive manufactures" draws special attention towards nations such as Lao PDR, Brunei and Myanmar which account for a small percent share for competitively positioned products, as is depicted in Table 8.3.

From India's point of view, weakly positioned Tier-II category accounts for the largest percent share in comparison with other product groupings, thereby revealing India's comparative disadvantage for products like 'base metal and articles' (72-83).

Table 8.3: RCA Profile for Low Skill and Technology Intensive Manufactures

(2001-2015)

Country	CP	TPL	EP (I)	EP (II)	WP (I)	WP (II)	Total
Brunei	11 (3.2)	1 (0.2)	7 (2.0)	202 (59.5)	2 (0.5)	116 (34.4)	339 (7.6)
Cambodia	11 (6.1)	1 (0.5)	5 (2.7)	100 (55.5)	1 (0.5)	62 (34.4)	180 (4.3)
India	84 (15.8)	75 (14.1)	44 (8.3)	111 (20.9)	46 (8.6)	170 (32.0)	530 (11.8)
Indonesia	49 (9.4)	14 (2.7)	18 (3.4)	161 (31.1)	24 (4.6)	251 (48.5)	517 (11.5)
Lao	6 (3.6)	1 (0.6)	5 (3.0)	90 (54.2)	0 (0.0)	64 (38.5)	166 (3.7)
Malaysia	75 (14.0)	17 (3.1)	43 (8.0)	220 (41.1)	23 (4.2)	157 (29.3)	535 (11.9)
Myanmar	5 (2.1)	0 (0.0)	5 (2.1)	228 (95.7)	0 (0.0)	0 (0.0)	238 (5.3)
Philippines	58 (14.0)	3 (0.7)	22 (5.3)	172 (41.5)	8 (1.9)	151 (36.4)	414 (9.2)
Singapore	45 (8.4)	26 (4.8)	34 (6.3)	177 (33.2)	30 (5.6)	220 (41.3)	532 (11.9)
Thailand	70 (13.5)	37 (7.1)	39 (7.5)	185 (35.8)	19 (3.6)	166 (32.1)	516 (11.5)
Vietnam	82 (16.6)	17 (3.4)	40 (8.1)	161 (32.7)	19 (3.8)	173 (35.1)	492 (11.0)

Note: Numbers in parenthesis are percentage shares in the respective product line.

Notes: CP = Competitive Positioned Products; TP = Threatened Products; EP (I) = Emerging Products Tier-I; EP (II) Emerging Products Tier-II; WP (I) = Weakly Positioned Products Tier-I and WP (II) = Weakly Positioned Products Tier-II.

Source: UNCOMTRADE; calculations by the researcher.

8.4 Medium Skill and Technology Intensive Manufactures

Out of a total of 7,497 product lines, 849 of them (11.32 percent of the total) have RCA index to be greater than unity and are still strengthening, hence positioning them under the "competitively positioned products" category. Table 8.4 encapsulates that Philippines constitutes the highest percent share of 24.05 for competitively positioned products followed by Vietnam with a 17.56 percent share. Malaysia and India stand at third and fourth position with their respective percentage share of 14.86 and 14.14 for competitively positioned products. Vietnam, Indonesia and Cambodia compose of a low percent share for competitively positioned products. Myanmar has the lowest percentage share of 0.81 in this category. Therefore, it is important for the Indian economy to gain better comparative advantage in this trending global trade. Hence, India should modify its production base for competitively positioned products and include 'machinery and mechanical appliances' (HS 84-85) to have more of a competitive edge.

As shown in the Table 8.4, Lao possesses the maximum percent share of 47.40 in weakly positioned products Tier-II category, followed by Indonesia with a 46.58 percent share and Singapore with the third highest percent share of 38.42. The large percent share in Tier-II product line indicates a larger degree of comparative disadvantage in this product grouping. India has the third lowest percentage share at 31.24 for 'plastic and rubber' (HS 39-40) and 'machinery and mechanical appliances' (84-85) followed by Cambodi . and Thailand with their respective percentage share of 29.11 and 25.18.

8.5 High Skill and Technology Intensive Manufactures

Under the competitively positioned products, the RCA index value is pegged to be greater than 1 and is still increasing exponentially. Table 8.5 enumerates that India constitutes the highest percentage share of 23.23 for 'chemical products' (28-38) followed by Cambodia with a 21.10

percentage share. Though the percent share margin is quite less between India and Cambodia, yet India out ways Cambodia in total number of product lines. Malaysia is positioned at the third place with a percentage share of 18.34. Lao, Vietnam and Brunei comprise of a low percentage share under competitively positioned product category as mentioned in Table 8.5. Myanmar constitutes the lowest percentage share of 3.22 depicting its low comparative advantage.

Table 8.4: RCA Profile for Medium Skill and Technology Intensive Manufactures

(2001-2015)

Country	CP	TPL	EP (I)	EP (II)	WP (I)	WP (II)	Total
Brunei	8 (1.3)	3 (0.4)	20 (3.2)	357 (58.6)	2 (0.3)	219 (35.9)	609 (8.1)
Cambodia	13 (5.4)	0 (0.0)	7 (2.9)	146 (61.6)	2 (0.8)	69 (29.1)	237 (3.1)
India	115 (14.1)	47 (5.7)	93 (11.4)	248 (30.5)	56 (6.8)	254 (31.2)	813 (10.8)
Indonesia	59 (7.9)	27 (3.2)	44 (5.3)	278 (33.9)	30 (3.6)	382 (46.5)	820 (10.9)
Lao	7 (1.5)	6 (1.3)	13 (2.9)	203 (45.8)	4 (0.9)	210 (47.4)	443 (5.9)
Malaysia	121 (14.8)	41 (5.0)	75 (9.2)	283 (34.7)	37 (4.5)	257 (31.5)	814 (10.8)
Myanmar	4 (0.8)	0 (0.0)	5 (1.0)	482 (98.1)	0 (0.0)	0 (0.0)	491 (6.5)
Philippines	203 (24.0)	24 (2.8)	32 (3.7)	305 (36.1)	4 (0.4)	276 (32.7)	844 (11.2)
Singapore	106 (12.8)	58 (7.0)	74 (8.9)	202 (24.4)	68 (8.2)	317 (38.4)	825 (11.0)
Thailand	143 (17.5)	56 (6.8)	94 (11.5)	281 (34.5)	35 (4.2)	205 (25.1)	814 (10.8)
Vietnam	70 (8.8)	20 (2.5)	45 (5.7)	368 (46.7)	11 (1.3)	273 (34.6)	787 (10.4)

Note: Numbers in parenthesis are percentage shares in the respective product line.

Notes: CP = Competitive Positioned Products; TP = Threatened Products; EP (I) = Emerging Products Tier-I; EP (II) Emerging Products Tier-II; WP (I) = Weakly Positioned Products Tier-I and WP (II) = Weakly Positioned Products Tier-II.

Source: UNCOMTRADE; calculations by the researcher.

Table 8.5: RCA Profile for High Skill and Technology Intensive Manufactures

(2001-2015)

Country	CP	TPL	EP (I)	EP (II)	WP (I)	WP (II)	Total
Brunei	23 (4.2)	1 (.1)	12 (2.2)	335 (62.6)	3 (0.5)	161 (30.0)	535 (5.8)
Cambodia	109 (21.1)	43 (8.3)	27 (5.2)	217 (42.0)	9 (1.7)	110 (21.3)	516 (5.6)
India	254 (21.2)	113 (9.4)	86 (7.1)	293 (24.4)	49 (4.0)	401 (33.5)	1196 (13.1)
Indonesia	87 (8.1)	52 (4.8)	48 (4.4)	375 (34.9)	27 (2.5)	458 (42.6)	1074 (11.7)
Lao	20 (7.2)	4 (1.4)	6 (2.1)	147 (53.2)	0 (0.0)	99 (35.8)	276 (3.0)
Malaysia	210 (18.3)	58 (5.0)	90 (7.8)	393 (34.3)	36 (3.1)	358 (31.2)	1145 (12.5)
Myanmar	16 (3.2)	0 (0.0)	3 (0.6)	477 (96.1)	0 (0.0)	0 (0.0)	496 (5.4)
Philippines	87 (12.5)	12 (1.7)	23 (3.3)	306 (44.2)	9 (1.3)	254 (36.7)	691 (7.5)
Singapore	182 (15.7)	115 (9.9)	102 (8.8)	263 (22.7)	92 (7.9)	403 (34.8)	1157 (12.6)
Thailand	171 (15.5)	63 (5.7)	81 (7.3)	444 (40.2)	30 (2.7)	313 (28.4)	1102 (12.0)
Vietnam	65 (6.9)	11 (1.1)	47 (5.0)	487 (51.9)	14 (1.4)	314 (33.4)	938 (10.2)

Note: Numbers in parenthesis are percentage shares in the respective product line.

Notes: CP = Competitive Positioned Products; TP = Threatened Products; EP (I) = Emerging Products Tier-I; EP (II) Emerging Products Tier-II; WP (I) = Weakly Positioned Products Tier-I and WP (II) = Weakly Positioned Products Tier-II.

Source: UNCOMTRADE; calculations by the researcher.

8.6 Mineral Fuels

RCA value for products should be greater than 1 and the mean RCA difference should be escalating, while positioning under "competitively positioned products" category. Table 8.6 explains that Thailand stands at the top most position with an enormous percentage share in competitively positioned products category at 54.17, followed by Philippines with a 27.81 percentage share and Vietnam stretching at third place with a 15.49 percent share in mineral fuel intensive commodities. India accounts for just 14.02 percent share for 'wood pulp products' (HS 47-49) and 'miscellaneous products' (HS 94-96) product grouping. Countries such as Indonesia, Malaysia and Lao constitute a low percentage share at 10.02 on an average. The profile of the "mineral fuel intensive manufactures" highlights that ASEAN members such as Brunei and Singapore comprise of the minimal percent share of 2.85 and 2.55 respectively for competitively positioned products which depicts lack of competitive advantage.

Table 8.6: RCA Profile for Mineral Fuel Manufactures (2001-2015)

Country	CP	TPL	EP (I)	EP (II)	WP (I)	WP (II)	Total
Brunei	3 (2.8)	0 (0.0)	3 (2.8)	61 (58.0)	0 (0.0)	38 (36.1)	105 (4.5)
Cambodia	3 (5.2)	1 (1.7)	1 (1.7)	30 (52.6)	1 (1.7)	21 (36.8)	57 (2.4)
India	25 (14.0)	16 (9.0)	14 (7.9)	50 (28.4)	5 (2.8)	66 (37.5)	176 (7.6)
Indonesia	20 (12.6)	11 (6.9)	5 (3.1)	36 (22.7)	9 (5.6)	77 (48.7)	158 (6.8)
Lao	7 (8.1)	2 (2.3)	1 (1.1)	38 (44.1)	0 (0.0)	38 (44.1)	86 (3.7)
Malaysia	16 (9.3)	8 (4.6)	17 (9.8)	67 (38.9)	5 (2.9)	59 (34.3)	172 (7.4)
Myanmar	5 (4.9)	0 (0.0)	1 (0.9)	96 (94.1)	0 (0.0)	0 (0.0)	102 (4.4)
Philippines	42 (27.8)	2 (1.3)	2 (1.3)	45 (29.8)	4 (2.6)	56 (37.0)	151 (6.5)
Singapore	21 (2.5)	11 (1.3)	10 (1.2)	44 (5.3)	3 (0.3)	734 (89.1)	823 (35.8)
Thailand	175 (54.1)	18 (5.5)	7 (2.1)	50 (15.4)	12 (3.7)	61 (18.8)	323 (14.0)
Vietnam	22 (15.4)	17 (11.9)	14 (9.8)	38 (26.7)	6 (4.2)	45 (31.6)	142 (6.1)

Note: Numbers in parenthesis are percentage shares in the respective product line.

Notes: CP = Competitive Positioned Products; TP = Threatened Products; EP (I) = Emerging Products Tier-I; EP (II) Emerging Products Tier-II; WP (I) = Weakly Positioned Products Tier-I and WP (II) = Weakly Positioned Products Tier-II.

Source: UNCOMTRADE; calculations by the researcher.

6.7 Conclusion

Amongst the six different industry levels, India exhibits a slow improvement in its competitiveness for non-fuel primary commodities such as 'vegetable products' (HS 06-14) and 'animal and animal products' (HS 01-05) with respect to the ASEAN members. The combined percentage share of India under competitively positioned and emerging products category under the RCA profile for non-fuel primary commodity is the lowest after Indonesia. ASEAN members such as Lao PDR, Malaysia, Myanmar, Philippines and Vietnam hold a higher combined percentage share, thereby demonstrating a marginal competitive edge of ASEAN members over India.

Under the low skill and technology intensive industry level, India displays a rising trend in its competitive positioning for 'base metals' (HS 72-83) and also a high percentage share in both competitively positioned and emerging product lines. However, India is still experiencing a competitive pressure from major ASEAN members such as Malaysia, Philippines, Singapore, Thailand and Vietnam. All these ASEAN members are registering a tremendously high percentage share in emerging products line, revealing a threat to the competitive position of India. India however demonstrates an improvement in its competitiveness for both medium and high skill and technology intensive manufactures such as 'machinery and mechanical appliances' (HS 84-85) and 'chemical products' (HS 28-38). On the contrary, India is constantly under the rising threat of increasing percentage share of the ASEAN members for emerging products, thereby revealing their ascending competitive stress. ASEAN members such as Malaysia, Philippines, Vietnam, Singapore and Thailand continue to be bigger threats in comparison with small and emerging members such as Brunei, Cambodia, Lao PDR and Myanmar.

Though India poses a gaining momentum in percentage change for mineral fuels under the 'miscellaneous products'

(HS 94-96) and 'wood pulp products' (HS 47-49) product lines having a RCA greater than 1, still approximately half of the percentage share of mineral fuel manufactures mirror under weakly positioned and threatened products. Nations such as Thailand, Philippines and Vietnam exhibit a large percentage share for competitively positioned products under the RCA profile for mineral fuels thereby depicting a higher competitive advantage of these nations over India.

Somewhat same phenomenon takes place under the resource intensive industry level where India portrays a high percentage share under the competitively positioned products and an increase in percentage change for product lines having RCA greater than 1. Still, India is losing its competitive advantage for 'textile and textile products' (HS 50-63) over ASEAN members such as Malaysia, Philippines and Vietnam. Countries such as Myanmar and Singapore are an emerging threat for India under resource intensive manufactures with a tremendously high percentage share under the emerging products category (Tier-I and Tier-II).

Therefore, to endure the competitiveness, India should focus on those industry levels that are reflecting a comparative advantage for the study period and should also take into consideration those industry levels where ASEAN members possess a higher percentage share for the emerging products. Thus, to gain competitiveness in this swiftly globalizing era, India should work more rigorously both at the micro and macro level.

9

India-ASEAN Trade: Competitive Positioning of Exports at Industry Level

9.1 Non-fuel Primary Commodities

The number of commodities under non-fuel primary product line in India's trade has increased from 949 to 1,012 during the period 2010-2015, depicting a total change of 7 percent. Also, there has been a rise in the number of products with comparative advantage greater than 1 from 215 in 2010 to 252 in 2015, depicting an overall jump of 17 percent. However, ASEAN member countries such as Philippines with a 45 percent and Thailand with a 39 percent change in product line with RCA greater than 1 exhibit a higher percentage change in the comparative advantage product line revealing a better competitive position with respect to India. Brunei and Myanmar show the highest percent change of 125 percent and 77 percent in comparative advantage product line. However, Brunei possesses quite a low volume of products in RCA>1 product line and Myanmar shows a 486 percent change in RCA<1 product line, thereby placing them amongst the least competitive economies. Singapore, the major ASEAN member, holds a negative comparative advantage of -3 percent following a rise of 24 percent change in comparative disadvantage product line (Table 9.1). Countries such as Vietnam, Malaysia, Lao and Cambodia also show a rise in comparative advantage in non-fuel primary commodities with an increase in percentage share in RCA greater than 1.

Table 9.1 shows the beginning of India's transformation from an import-competing country to one, positioning itself as an export market for non-fuel primary commodities. In spite of existence of various stumbling blocks, India demonstrates a slow improvement in competitive performance for non-fuel primary commodities.

Table 9.1: Profile for Non-fuel Primary Commodities (2010-2015)

Country	Product line with RCA>1			Product line with RCA<1		
	2010	2015	Percent Change	2010	2015	Percent Change
Brunei	4 (2.5)	9 (05)	125	153 (97)	170 (95)	11
Cambodia	43 (35)	58 (30)	35	80 (65)	134 (70)	68
India	215 (23)	252 (25)	17	734 (77)	760 (75)	4
Indonesia	186 (27)	210 (32)	13	513 (73)	456 (68)	-11
Lao	85 (47)	93 (49)	9	94 (53)	97 (51)	3
Malaysia	131 (16)	178 (19)	36	676 (84)	763 (81)	13
Myanmar	52 (59)	92 (30)	77	36 (41)	211 (70)	486
Philippines	116 (27)	168 (33)	45	317 (73)	345 (67)	9
Singapore	77 (9)	75 (8)	-3	746 (91)	922 (92)	24
Thailand	195 (24)	271 (27)	39	622 (76)	738 (73)	19
Vietnam	194 (30)	221 (32)	14	462 (70)	476 (68)	3

contd...

Country	Total No. of Products		
	2010	2015	Percent Change
Brunei	157	179	14
Cambodia	123	192	56
India	949	1012	7
Indonesia	699	666	-5
Lao	179	190	6
Malaysia	807	941	17
Myanmar	88	303	244
Philippines	433	513	18
Singapore	823	997	21
Thailand	817	1009	24
Vietnam	656	697	6

Note: Numbers in parenthesis are percentage change in the respective product line.

Source: UNCOMTRADE; calculations by the researcher.

9.2 Resource Intensive Manufactures

The overall position of India in the resource intensive manufactures does not exhibit a huge improvement from 2010 to 2015. While an increase of mere 5 percent could be observed in the comparative advantage category, with the decrease in total number of product lines from 1,198 to 1,190, almost 60 percent of the product line exhibits a comparative disadvantage in 2015. ASEAN members such as Indonesia and Lao display a higher level of comparative disadvantage with the negative percent change of -1 and -23 in the RCA greater than 1 and simultaneously a decline in the total number of products by 1 percent.

Nations such as Malaysia and Philippines demonstrate a higher level of enhancement in the competitive positioning in comparison with other ASEAN members. Both the economies represent an increase of 514 percent and 22 percent in the comparative advantage product line, followed by an increase in total products from 274 in 2010 to 1,671 in 2015. Based on this, it can be inferred that Malaysia is gaining a high momentum in resource intensive manufactures at the industry level. Lastly, nations such as Brunei, Cambodia, Singapore and Vietnam are holding their comparative disadvantage with a high percent share in product line with RCA less than 1 for 2015 which can be observed from Table 9.2. One can easily infer that India's competitive positioning in resource intensive manufactures has not made an enormous addition. Hence, India should formulate vibrant trade policies to achieve a sustainable competitiveness in the particular industry level.

9.3 Low Skill and Technology Intensive Manufactures

Industry level profile of low skill and technology intensive manufactures has been illustrated in Table 9.3. This industry level examines the comprehensive outlook for India with respect to other ASEAN members. India portrays a rise in comparative advantage with a 9 percent change in product line with RCA greater than unity and also a negative change of 4 percent in RCA less than 1 product line with a 71 percent share percent in 2015.

On the contrary, major ASEAN members such as

Malaysia, Singapore and Indonesia hold fewer percentage share change of 15, 13 and 10 percent respectively in 2015 for product line RCA greater than 1 and exhibit a higher percentage share in competitively disadvantage product line with their respective percent share of 85, 87 and 88 percent in 2015, thereby revealing these nations to be less competitive in comparison to India.

Table 9.2: Profile for Resource Intensive Manufactures (2010-2015)

Country	Product line with RCA>1			Product line with RCA<1		
	2010	2015	Percent Change	2010	2015	Percent Change
Brunei	8 (3)	15 (5)	88	261 (97)	276 (95)	6
Cambodia	20 (14)	32 (14)	60	119 (86)	192 (86)	61
India	455 (38)	479 (40)	5	743 (62)	711 (60)	-4
Indonesia	358 (36)	353 (36)	-1	634 (64)	626 (64)	-1
Lao	94 (33)	72 (24)	-23	187 (67)	232 (76)	24
Malaysia	124 (45)	761 (46)	514	150 (55)	910 (54)	507
Myanmar	35 (55)	139 (31)	297	29 (45)	310 (69)	969
Philippines	180 (29)	219 (31)	22	448 (71)	487 (69)	9
Singapore	46 (5)	56 (5)	22	931 (95)	1054 (95)	13
Thailand	275 (28)	300 (29)	9	712 (72)	737 (71)	4
Vietnam	431 (49)	432 (44)	0	450 (51)	540 (56)	20

contd...

Country	Total No. of Products		
	2010	2015	Percent Change
Brunei	269	291	8
Cambodia	139	224	61
India	1198	1190	-1
Indonesia	992	979	-1
Lao	281	304	8
Malaysia	274	1671	509
Myanmar	64	449	602
Philippines	628	706	12
Singapore	977	1110	14
Thailand	987	1037	5
Vietnam	881	972	10

Note: Numbers in parenthesis are percentage change in the respective product line.

Source: UNCOMTRADE; calculations by the researcher.

Vietnam displays the best competitive positioning amongst the ASEAN members with a higher percent change of 28 in RCA greater than unity and a decline in percentage share in competitive disadvantage product line with a share of 78 percent in 2015, down from 82 percent in 2010. Brunei, Cambodia, Laos and Myanmar are the least competitive economies in the low skill and technology intensive manufactures.

Table 9.3: Profile for Low Skill and Technology Intensive Manufactures

(2001-2015)

Country	Product line with RCA>1			Product line with RCA<1		
	2010	2015	Percent Change	2010	2015	Percent Change
Brunei	12 (6)	18 (9)	50	197 (94)	186 (91)	-6
Cambodia	6 (8)	11 (9)	83	65 (92)	109 (91)	68
India	135 (27)	147 (29)	9	373 (73)	358 (71)	-4
Indonesia	48 (12)	52 (12)	8	365 (88)	376 (88)	3
Lao	3 (6)	6 (10)	100	46 (94)	52 (90)	13
Malaysia	69 (15)	74 (15)	7	385 (85)	415 (85)	8
Myanmar	2 (20)	6 (5)	200	8 (80)	106 (95)	1225
Philippines	22 (10)	45 (17)	105	193 (90)	226 (83)	17
Singapore	63 (14)	62 (13)	-2	394 (86)	413 (87)	5
Thailand	85 (19)	106 (20)	25	374 (81)	421 (80)	13
Vietnam	74 (19)	95 (22)	28	326 (82)	346 (78)	6

contd...

Country	Total No. of Product Lines		
	2010	2015	Percent Change
Brunei	209	204	-2
Cambodia	71	120	69
India	508	505	-1
Indonesia	413	428	4
Lao	49	58	18
Malaysia	454	489	8
Myanmar	10	112	1020
Philippines	215	271	26
Singapore	457	475	4
Thailand	459	527	15
Vietnam	400	441	10

Note: Numbers in parenthesis are percentage change in the respective product line.

Source: UNCOMTRADE; calculations by the researcher.

9.4 Medium Skill and Technology Intensive Manufactures

Under the medium skill and technology intensive manufactures, India exhibits a drive from low to moderately advantageous competitive economy with a 38 percent change in competitive positioned product line with RCA index greater than 1 and shows a negative trend in less competitive positioned products from 666 to 616 product items, thereby depicting India's comparative advantage in comparison with the entire ASEAN members in medium skill and technology intensive manufactures as depicted in Table 9.4.

On the contrary, ASEAN members Thailand and Philippines are also positioned as emerging competitive economies in medium skill and technology intensive manufactures. Philippines exhibits a 116 percent change in competitive positioned products with RCA greater than 1 and shows a decline in percentage share in less competitive positioned products from 88 percent in 2010 to 82 percent in 2015. Similarly, Thailand also demonstrates an increase of 31 percent change in competitively positioned products and 71 percent share in less competitive positioned product line.

ASEAN member such as Myanmar, Brunei, Indonesia and Lao PDR turn up to be the least competitive economies in medium skill and technology intensive manufactures despite an increase in total number of products. Myanmar however, shows an enormous increase from 6 in 2010 to 234 in 2015 with a high percentage share in less competitively positioned products with RCA less than 1 with their respective percentage values as depicted in Table 9.4. Lastly, Malaysia exhibits no change in percentage share in both the product lines. Share percent in RCA greater than 1 was 16 percent in 2010, which remained more or less the same in 2015, thereby revealing no gain in competitive advantage.

9.5 High Skill and Technology Intensive Manufactures

Table 9.5 presents a description of high skill and technology intensive manufactures and reveals that India possesses a partial cc nparative advantage in a particular industry level with an increase from 290 products in 2010 to 350 products in 2015, a 21 percent change in competitive positioned product line having RCA greater than 1 and also a decline in less competitive products from 73 percent to 68 percent.

Table 9.4: Profile for Medium Skill and Technology Intensive Manufactures

(2001-2015)

Country	Product line with RCA>1			Product line with RCA<1		
	2010	2015	Percent Change	2010	2015	Percent Change
Brunei	10 (3)	26 (6)	160	387 (97)	388 (94)	0
Cambodia	8 (8)	17 (32)	113	87 (92)	36 (68)	-59
India	138 (17)	190 (24)	38	666 (83)	616 (76)	-8
Indonesia	76 (11)	74 (10)	-3	634 (89)	647 (90)	2
Lao	25 (16)	12 (7)	-52	134 (84)	165 (93)	23
Malaysia	120 (16)	145 (16)	21	612 (84)	753 (84)	23
Myanmar	0 (0)	7 (3)	-	6 (100)	227 (97)	3683
Philippines	43 (12)	93 (18)	116	318 (88)	438 (82)	38
Singapore	141 (19)	159 (20)	13	599 (81)	623 (80)	4
Thailand	170 (23)	223 (29)	31	566 (77)	556 (71)	-2
Vietnam	84 (14)	76 (11)	-10	530 (86)	603 (89)	14

contd...

Country	Total No. of Product Lines		
	2010	2015	Percent Change
Brunei	397	414	4
Cambodia	95	53	-44
India	804	806	0
Indonesia	710	721	2
Lao	159	177	11
Malaysia	732	898	23
Myanmar	6	234	3800
Philippines	361	531	47
Singapore	740	782	6
Thailand	736	779	6
Vietnam	614	679	11

Note: Numbers in parenthesis are percentage change in the respective product line.

Source: UNCOMTRADE; calculations by the researcher.

However, ASEAN members such as Cambodia and

Philippines are the rapidly emerging economies in the high skill and technology intensive manufactures. Nations such as Brunei, Myanmar and Vietnam are least competitively advantageous with a heavy percentage share in less competitively positioned product line possessing RCA value to be less than 1 with their respective values pegged at 94, 90 and 87 percent during the year 2015.

Table 9.5: Profile for High Skill and Technology Intensive Manufactures

(2010-2015)

Country	Product line with RCA>1			Product line with RCA<1		
	2010	2015	Percent Change	2010	2015	Percent Change
Brunei	18 (4)	26 (6)	44	387 (96)	388 (94)	0
Cambodia	93 (36)	158 (42)	70	162 (64)	217 (58)	34
India	290 (27)	350 (32)	21	802 (73)	754 (68)	-6
Indonesia	121 (16)	120 (15)	-1	659 (84)	670 (85)	2
Lao	12 (15)	19 (18)	58	67 (85)	88 (82)	31
Malaysia	177 (20)	213 (24)	20	724 (80)	683 (76)	-6
Myanmar	4 (25)	16 (10)	300	12 (75)	147 (90)	1125
Philippines	94 (21)	171 (33)	82	348 (79)	343 (67)	-1
Singapore	257 (26)	248 (27)	4	722 (74)	760 (73)	-5
Thailand	180 (20)	252 (27)	40	701 (80)	679 (73)	-3
Vietnam	65 (11)	88 (13)	35	545 (87)	608 (87)	12

contd...

Country	Total No. of Product Lines		
	2010	2015	Percent Change
Brunei	405	414	2
Cambodia	255	375	47
India	1092	1104	1
Indonesia	780	790	1
Lao	79	107	35
Malaysia	901	896	-1
Myanmar	16	163	918
Philippines	442	514	16
Singapore	979	1008	3
Thailand	881	931	6
Vietnam	610	696	14

Note: Numbers in parenthesis are percentage change in the respective product line.

Source: UNCOMTRADE; calculations by the researcher.

9.6 Mineral Fuel Manufactures

Total number of reported product lines for India under mineral fuel in 2010 was 163, out of which 30 products were competitively positioned, having a share of 18 percent. By 2015, the percent share increased to 25 percent with 41 products. Also, the negative change of 8 percent in less competitively positioned product line with RCA less than 1 show that India is gaining competitive momentum in mineral fuel manufactures.

On the contrary, ASEAN countries such as Philippines, Thailand and Vietnam are emerging economies in mineral fuel manufactures and hold a higher comparative advantage in comparison with other ASEAN members. Philippines exhibited an 81 percent change in competitively positioned product line with an increase in total product line from 88 in 2010 to 105 in 2015.

Similarly, Thailand also demonstrated an increase in competitively positioned products from 35 in 2010 to 44 in 2015; a 26 percent change in competitively positioned products with RCA greater than 1 and a 72 percent share in less competitively positioned product line. Vietnam displayed a 33 percent share in product line having RCA value greater than 1, with total number of products increasing from 112 to 121 with an 8 percent change.

As per Table 9.6, Singapore also demonstrated a slow rise in mineral fuel manufactures with a high percentage change of 40 percent followed by a decrease in the percentage share from 86 percent in 2010 to 82 percent in 2015 under the less competitively positioned products having RCA less than 1. On the other hand, countries such as Brunei and Malaysia demonstrated a mere one percent change in competitively positioned product line with RCA greater than 1.

Lastly, the rest of ASEAN members such as Cambodia, Indonesia, Lao and Myanmar held a comparative disadvantage in mineral fuel manufactures with a high percentage share in less competitively positioned product line having RCA value to be less than 1 with their respective values standing at 93, 74, 90 and 90 percent for the year 2015. These nations also exhibited a negative percentage change for competitively positioned products having RCA greater than 1 with their respective values pegged at -50, -6, and -43 percent.

Table 9.6: Profile for Mineral Fuel Manufactures (2010-2015)

Country	Product line with RCA>1			Product line with RCA<1		
	2010	2015	Percent Change	2010	2015	Percent Change
Brunei	2 (3)	2 (4)	0	58 (97)	51 (96)	-12
Cambodia	4 (18)	2 (7)	-50	18 (82)	26 (93)	44
India	30 (18)	41 (25)	37	133 (82)	123 (75)	-8
Indonesia	36 (26)	34 (26)	-6	101 (74)	98 (74)	-3
Lao	7 (19)	4 (10)	-43	30 (81)	36 (90)	20
Malaysia	20 (14)	23 (15)	15	119 (86)	132 (85)	11
Myanmar	3 (38)	6 (10)	100	5 (63)	56 (90)	1020
Philippines	16 (18)	29 (28)	81	72 (82)	76 (72)	6
Singapore	20 (14)	28 (18)	40	123 (86)	127 (82)	3
Thailand	35 (24)	44 (28)	26	110 (76)	115 (72)	5
Vietnam	37 (33)	40 (33)	8	75 (67)	81 (67)	8

contd...

Country	Total No. of Product Lines		
	2010	2015	Percent Change
Brunei	60	53	-12
Cambodia	22	28	28
India	163	164	1
Indonesia	137	132	-4
Lao	37	40	8
Malaysia	139	155	12
Myanmar	8	62	675
Philippines	88	105	19
Singapore	143	155	8
Thailand	145	159	10
Vietnam	112	121	8

Note: Numbers in parenthesis are percentage change in the respective product line.
Source: UNCOMTRADE; calculations by the researcher.

9.7 Conclusion

Analysis of the study leads to interesting and insightful

observations. Amongst the six different industry levels, India exhibits a slow improvement in its competitiveness for non-fuel primary commodities such as 'vegetable products' (HS 06-14) and 'animal and animal products' (HS 01-05) with respect to other ASEAN members. The combined percentage share of India under competitively positioned and emerging products under RCA profile for non-fuel primary commodities is the lowest after Indonesia. ASEAN members such as Lao PDR, Malaysia, Myanmar, Philippines and Vietnam hold a higher combined percentage share, thereby depicting a marginal competitive edge of these ASEAN members over India.

Under the low skill and technology intensive industry level, India displays a rising trend in its competitive positioning for 'base metals' (HS 72-83) and also a high percentage share in both competitively positioned and emerging product line. However, India is still experiencing a competitive pressure from major ASEAN members such as Malaysia, Philippines, Singapore, Thailand and Vietnam. All these ASEAN members are registering a tremendously high percentage share in emerging product line, revealing a threat to the competitive position of India.

India has demonstrated an improvement in its competitiveness for both medium and high skill and technology intensive manufactures such as 'machinery and mechanical appliances' (HS 84-85) and 'chemical products' (HS 28-38). Both the industry levels display an escalating percentage change in product line having RCA value to be greater than 1. On the contrary, India is constantly under the rising threat of increasing percentage share of ASEAN members for emerging products, thereby revealing their ascending competitive stress. ASEAN members such as Malaysia, Philippines, Vietnam, Singapore and Thailand appear to be bigger threats in comparison with small and emerging members such as Brunei, Cambodia, Lao PDR and Myanmar.

Although India poses a gaining momentum in percentage change for mineral fuel industry level for 'miscellaneous products' (HS 94-96) and 'wood pulp products' (HS 47-49) product line having RCA greater than 1, yet approximately half of the percentage share of mineral fuel manufactures mirrors a weak position. Nations such as Thailand, Philippines and Vietnam exhibit a large percentage share for competitively positioned products under the RCA profile for mineral fuels thereby depicting a higher competitive advantage of these nations over India. Somewhat same phenomenon also takes place under the resource intensive industry level, where India portrays a higher percentage share under the competitively positioned products, still India is losing its competitive advantage for 'textile and textile products' (HS 50-63) over ASEAN members such as Malaysia, Philippines and Vietnam. Countries such as Myanmar and Singapore are an emerging threat for India under the resource intensive manufactures with a tremendously high percentage share under the emerging products category (Tier-I and Tier-II).

Therefore, to endure its competitiveness, India should focus on those industry levels which reflect a comparative advantage and should also take into consideration those industry levels where ASEAN members possess a higher percentage share for emerging products. Thus, to gain competitiveness in this swiftly globalizing era, India should work more rigorously both at the micro and the macro level.

10

India-ASEAN Trade: Industry-wise Import Dependency

10.1 Non-fuel Primary Commodity

Out of the 12,142 HS 6 digit level product line, 2,079 of them (17.12 percent of the total) possess a RID value to be greater than unity and the average RID difference is still increasing, thereby placing them under the "rising dependence" category. Table 10.1 explains that Brunei constituted a 36.49 percent share in rising dependence product line followed by Philippines with a 25.97 percent share and Malaysia sketching a 23.67 percent share. The RID profile of "non-fuel primary products" highlights the headways made by India with just a 10.17 percent share, positioning it to be the lowest followed by Lao PDR with a mere share of 10.66 percent making these economies highly advantageous in comparison with nations such as Thailand, Singapore and Indonesia. Therefore, it is important for the Indian economy to gain more advantage under the growing global trade by reducing its dependence on other nations, for 'vegetable products' (HS 06-14) and 'mineral products' (HS 25-27).

The emerging threatened products are divided into two groups to draw a distinction between two types of product lines: (a) Tier-I and (b) Tier-II. In the first category of Tier-I, there are a total of 875 product lines that depict a percentage of 7.20 of the total product line. In this category, India constitutes least percent share of just 4.90 for 'vegetable products' (HS 06-14) followed by Cambodia with a 4.97 share percent and Indonesia standing with a third lowest percent share of 4.99. The profile highlights that Singapore and Malaysia depicted the highest percent share in Tier-I category with their respective percent values at 10.42 and 10.86. The figures evident in Table 10.1 highlight that Indian manufacturing is moving towards self-sufficiency in emerging threatened products Tier-I category.

The profile highlights that there is a need for determined efforts to ensure that India sustains and strengthens its import dependency by increasing its percent share in particular product line.

Table 10.1: RID Profile for Non-Fuel Primary Commodities (2001-2015)

Country	RD	ET (I)	ET (II)	LT (I)	LT (II)	RI	Total
Brunei	358 (36.4)	65 (6.6)	250 (25.4)	29 (2.9)	209 (21.0)	70 (7.1)	981 (8.0)
Cambodia	91 (11.3)	40 (4.9)	415 (51.6)	14 (1.7)	222 (27.6)	22 (2.7)	804 (6.6)
India	110 (10.1))	53 (4.9)	410 (37.9)	53 (4.9)	368 (34.7)	87 (8.0)	1081 (8.9)
Indonesia	154 (12.6)	61 (4.9)	417 (34.1)	53 (4.3)	425 (34.0)	112 (9.1)	1222 (10.0)
Lao	90 (10.6)	52 (6.1)	370 (43.8)	26 (3.0)	239 (28.3)	67 (7.9)	844 (6.9)
Malaysia	316 (23.6)	145 (10.8)	492 (36.8)	54 (4.0)	250 (18.7)	78 (5.8)	1335 (10.9)
Myanmar	168 (16.7)	65 (6.4)	768 (76.7)	-	-	-	1001 (8.2)
Philippines	273 (25.9)	79 (7.5)	347 (33.0)	37 (3.5)	268 (25.5)	47 (4.4)	1051 (8.6)
Singapore	165 (12.7)	135 (10.4)	478 (36.9)	28 (2.1)	465 (35.9)	24 (1.8)	1295 (10.6)
Thailand	172 (13.1)	111 (8.4)	532 (40.6)	47 (3.5)	347 (26.5)	99 (7.5)	1308 (10.7)
Vietnam	182 (14.9)	69 (5.6)	453 (3.1)	42 (3.4)	384 (31.4)	90 (7.3)	1220 (10.0)

Note: Numbers in parenthesis are percentage shares in the respective product line.

Notes: RD = Rising Dependence Products; RI = Rising Independence Products; ET (I) = Emerging Threatened Products Tier-I; ET (II) Emerging Threatened Products Tier-II; LT (I) = Less Threatened Products Tier-I and LT (II) = Less Threatened Products Tier-II.

Source: UNCOMTRADE; calculations by the researcher.

10.2 Resource Intensive Manufactures

"Rising dependence" product category possesses a RID value greater than unity and the average RID difference is still increasing. Table 10.2 clearly signifies that Myanmar constitutes the highest percent share of 37.67 in rising dependence products followed by Brunei with a 34.00 percent share and Vietnam sketching at third place with a 27.23 percent share in rising dependence product line. The profile of the "resource intensive manufactures" highlight that nations such as Singapore and India both account for a low percent share for the particular product line. India holds a percentage share of 09.33 for 'textile and textile products' (HS 50-63).

Table 10.2: RID Profile for Resource Intensive Manufactures (2001-2015)

Country	RD	ET (I)	ET (II)	LT (I)	LT (II)	RI	Total
Brunei	355 (34.0)	73 (6.9)	271 (25.9)	28 (2.6)	221 (21.1)	96 (9.1)	1044 (8.0)
Cambodia	180 (18.9)	44 (4.6)	332 (35.0)	34 (3.5)	306 (32.2)	52 (5.4)	948 (7.2)
India	117 (9.3)	73 (5.8)	543 (43.3)	45 (3.5)	436 (34.7)	39 (3.1)	1253 (9.6)
Indonesia	333 (26.8)	122 (9.8)	399 (32.1)	46 (3.7)	291 (23.4)	49 (3.9)	1240 (9.5)
Lao	210 (19.7)	59 (5.5)	294 (27.6)	62 (5.8)	339 (31.8)	101 (9.4)	1065 (8.1)
Malaysia	185 (16.1)	131 (11.4)	408 (35.5)	78 (6.8)	292 (25.4)	53 (4.6)	1147 (8.8)
Myanmar	445 (37.6)	147 (12.4)	589 (49.8)	-	-	-	1181 (9.0)
Philippines	336 (24.7)	118 (8.6)	426 (31.3)	57 (4.2)	365 (26.8)	55 (4.0)	1357 (10.4)
Singapore	115 (9.3)	117 (9.4)	324 (26.2)	43 (3.4)	620 (50.2)	15 (1.2)	1234 (9.4)
Thailand	154 (12.3)	111 (8.8)	466 (37.2)	108 (8.6)	316 (25.2)	97 (7.7)	1252 (9.6)
Vietnam	338 (27.2)	72 (5.8)	338 (27.2)	47 (3.7)	274 (22.0)	172 (13.8)	1241 (9.5)

Note: Numbers in parenthesis are percentage shares in the respective product line.

Notes: RD = Rising Dependence Products; RI = Rising Independence Products; ET (I) = Emerging Threatened Products Tier-I; ET (II) Emerging Threatened Products Tier-II; LT (I) = Less Threatened Products Tier-I and LT (II) = Less Threatened Products Tier-II.

Source: UNCOMTRADE; calculations by the researcher.

10.3 Low Skill and Technology Intensive Manufacturing

Of the total 5,569 HS 6 digit level product line, 1,385 of them (24.86 percent of the total) possess a RID value to be greater than unity thereby placing them under "rising dependence" product category. Table 10.3 clearly illustrates that Brunei stands highest with a 41.50 percent share in low skill and technology intensive manufactures accompanied by Myanmar at the second position with a 39.96 percent share and Indonesia sketching at the third position with a 29.67 percent share in low skill and technology intensive manufactures. The RID profile draws special attention towards nations such as India which accounts with a least percent share of 14.23 for 'base metal and articles' (HS 72-83) accompanied by Cambodia and Singapore with a low percent share of 15.86 and 17.42 respectively under the rising dependence product category.

The RID profile emphasizes that there exists a lower percentage share under the rising independence product line, which could be an alarming situation for the competitiveness in coming years for 'transport equipment' (HS 86-89) and 'base metal and articles' (HS 72-83) for the Indian import sector.

Table 10.3: RID Profile for Low Skill and Technology Intensive Manufactures

(2010-2015)

Country	RD	ET (I)	ET (II)	LT (I)	LT (II)	RI	Total
Brunei	193 (41.5)	26 (5.5)	79 (16.9)	28 (6.0)	88 (18.9)	51 (10.9)	465 (8.3)
Cambodia	69 (15.8)	29 (6.6)	154 (35.4)	17 (3.9)	137 (31.4)	29 (6.6)	435 (7.8)
India	75 (14.2)	57 (10.9)	163 (30.9)	37 (7.0)	149 (28.2)	46 (8.7)	527 (9.4)
Indonesia	157 (29.6)	58 (10.8)	83 (15.6)	55 (10.3)	92 (17.3)	84 (15.8)	529 (9.4)
Lao	110 (22.8)	45 (9.3)	120 (24.9)	23 (4.7)	130 (27.0)	53 (11.0)	481 (8.6)
Malaysia	135 (25.5)	77 (14.5)	121 (22.8)	44 (8.3)	77 (14.5)	52 (9.8)	529 (9.4)
Myanmar	201 (39.9)	85 (16.8)	122 (24.2)	-	-	-	503 (9.0)

contd...

Philippines	105 (19.4)	98 (18.1)	123 (22.8)	16 (2.9)	135 (25.0)	15 (2.7)	539 (9.6)
Singapore	88 (17.4)	66 (13.0)	124 (24.5)	36 (7.1)	195 (38.6)	5 (0.9)	505 (9.0)
Thailand	129 (24.2)	77 (14.5)	125 (23.5)	31 (5.8)	114 (21.4)	49 (9.2)	531 (9.5)
Vietnam	123 (23.4)	49 (9.3)	126 (24)	44 (5.3)	138 (26.2)	85 (16.1)	525 (9.4)

Note: Numbers in parenthesis are percentage shares in the respective product line.

Notes: RD = Rising Dependence Products; RI = Rising Independence Products; ET (I) = Emerging Threatened Products Tier-I; ET (II) Emerging Threatened Products Tier-II; LT (I) = Less Threatened Products Tier-I and LT (II) = Less Threatened Products Tier-II.

Source: UNCOMTRADE; calculations by the researcher.

10.4 Medium Skill and Technology Intensive Manufactures

"Rising dependence products" constitute a RID index to be greater than unity and is still strengthening the import dependence. Table 10.4 encapsulates that Brunei constitutes the highest percentage share of 52.51 followed by Myanmar at 45.55 percent share and Indonesia and Vietnam standing at third and fourth position with their respective percentage share of 40.00 and 28.80 for the particular product line. The RID profile of the "medium skill and technology intensive manufactures" also spotlight towards those economies which account for a small percentage share. India portrays a low percent share of 16.30 for 'machinery and mechanical appliances' (HS 84-85) followed by Singapore and Lao PDR with their percentage share of 18.03 and 23.68 respectively for rising dependence products, thereby signifying a low import dependency.

The RID profile for medium skill and technology intensive manufactures highlights that India should thrive for more percent share in particular product category for 'plastics and rubber' (HS 39-40) and 'machinery and mechanical appliances' (84-85) to have less of import dependence from ASEAN members.

10.5 High Skill and Technology Intensive Manufactures

Under "rising dependence" product category, the RID

indices value happens to be greater than 1 and is still ramping exponentially. Table 10.5 enumerates that Brunei accounts for the highest percentage share of 32.87 followed by Philippines with a 31.15 percentage share. India and Thailand constitute the somewhat same percent share of 21.54 on an average, thereby depicting that India accounts largely for 'chemical products' (HS 28-38) imports. Hence, concerted efforts and determined policies should be framed to reduce India's percentage share in this category.

Table 10.4: RID Profile for Medium Skill and Technology Intensive Manufactures

(2001-2015)

Country	RD	ET (I)	ET (II)	LT (I)	LT (II)	RI	Total
Brunei	407 (52.5)	63 (8.1)	156 (20.1)	20 (2.5)	95 (12.2)	34 (4.3)	775 (8..7)
Cambodia	190 (24.1)	69 (8.7)	234 (29.6)	39 (4.9)	216 (27.4)	40 (5.0)	788 (8.8)
India	134 (16.3)	107 (13.0)	200 (24.3)	104 (12.6)	194 (23.6)	83 (10.0)	820 (9.2)
Indonesia	328 (40.0)	120 (14.6)	93 (11.3)	62 (7.5)	77 (9.3)	140 (17.0)	822 (9.2)
Lao	184 (23.6)	82 (10.5)	168 (21.6)	46 (5.9)	205 (26.3)	92 (11.8)	777 (8.7)
Malaysia	230 (28.6)	137 (17.0)	155 (19.3)	77 (9.5)	84 (10.4)	120 (14.9)	803 (9.0)
Myanmar	369 (45.5)	153 (18.8)	288 (35.5)	-	-	-	810 (9.1)
Philippines	227 (26.9)	158 (18.7)	265 (31.4)	31 (3.6)	132 (15.6)	29 (3.4)	842 (9.4)
Singapore	147 (18.0)	111 (13.6)	133 (16.3)	85 (10.4)	297 (36.4)	42 (5.1)	815 (9.1)
Thailand	220 (27.0)	134 (16.4)	129 (15.8)	75 (9.2)	118 (14.4)	138 (16.9)	814 (9.1)
Vietnam	233 (28.8)	98 (12.1)	96 (11.8)	70 (8.6)	138 (17.0)	174 (21.5)	809 (9.1)

Note: Numbers in parenthesis are percentage shares in the respective product line.

Notes: RD = Rising Dependence Products; RI = Rising Independence Products; ET (I) = Emerging Threatened Products Tier-I; ET (II) Emerging Threatened Products Tier-II; LT (I) = Less Threatened Products Tier-I and LT (II) = Less Threatened Products Tier-II.

Source: UNCOMTRADE; calculations by the researcher.

The RID profile also draws special attention towards countries which constitute a small percentage share such as Lao PDR and Cambodia, depicting a low degree of import dependency for high skill and technology products.

Rising independence product lines depict import dependence greater than 1, but have experienced a negative share during 2001-2015. Table 10.5 clearly illustrates that Indonesia sketches the highest percent share which accounts to be 21.36 followed by Thailand for 15.86 percent share.

Table 10.5: RID Profile for High Skill and Technology Intensive Manufactures

(2001-2015)

Country	RD	ET (I)	ET (II)	LT (I)	LT (II)	RI	Total
Brunei	312 (32.8)	72 (7.5)	261 (27.5)	31 (3.2)	222 (23.3)	51 (5.3)	949 (7.7)
Cambodia	96 (10.4)	72 (7.8)	350 (37.9)	21 (2.2)	352 (38.1)	32 (3.4)	923 (7.5)
India	258 (21.7)	125 (10.5)	217 (18.3)	100 (8.4)	323 (27.2)	161 (13.5)	1184 (9.7)
Indonesia	251 (20.9)	133 (11.1)	237 (19.7)	95 (7.9)	226 (18.8)	256 (21.3)	1198 (9.8)
Lao	88 (10.2)	42 (4.9)	345 (40.3)	28 (3.2)	301 (35.1)	52 (6.0)	856 (7.0)
Malaysia	320 (26.6)	192 (15.9)	232 (19.3)	92 (7.6)	204 (16.9)	162 (13.4)	1202 (9.8)
Myanmar	259 (24.2)	162 (15.1)	645 (60.5)	-	-	-	1066 (8.7)
Philippines	391 (31.1)	143 (11.3)	262 (20.8)	92 (7.3)	291 (23.1)	76 (6.0)	1255 (10.3)
Singapore	241 (20.4)	149 (12.6)	202 (17.1)	115 (9.7)	393 (33.3)	80 (6.7)	1180 (9.6)
Thailand	252 (21.2)	153 (12.9)	201 (16.9)	109 (9.1)	282 (23.7)	188 (15.8)	1185 (9.7)
Vietnam	225 (19.1)	130 (11.0)	242 (20.5)	105 (8.9)	312 (26.4)	164 (13.9)	1178 (9.6)

Note: Numbers in parenthesis are percentage shares in the respective product line.

Notes: RD = Rising Dependence Products; RI = Rising Independence Products; ET (I) = Emerging Threatened Products Tier-I; ET (II) Emerging Threatened Products Tier-II; LT (I) = Less Threatened Products Tier-I and LT (II) = Less Threatened Products Tier-II.

Source: UNCOMTRADE; calculations by the researcher.

10.6 Mineral Fuel Manufactures

Out of a of 1,862 HS 6 digit level product line, 382 of them (20.51 percent of the total) maintain a RID value of greater than 1 and the mean RID difference is still escalating, hence positioning them under the "rising dependence product" category. Table 10.6 explains clearly that Brunei hold an enormous percentage share at 45.69, followed by Myanmar with a 29.94 percentage share and Philippines positioned at third place with a 26.08 percent share. India accounts for the lowest percent share of 5.11 for 'wood pulp products' (HS 47-49) product grouping.

The RID profile of "mineral fuel intensive manufactures" spotlights that ASEAN members such as Vietnam, Thailand, Malaysia and Singapore comprise of a higher percent share in the particular product group, which explains the rise in import dependence by the ASEAN members.

Under the 'emerging threatened products tier-I category', there are a total of 177 product lines which depicts a low percentage share of 9.50 out of the total 1,862 product lines. In this category, India constitutes the lowest percentage share of 3.97 for 'miscellaneous products' (HS 94-96) and 'wood pulp products' (HS 47-49) followed by Vietnam with a 5.52 percent share standing at the second lowest position and Indonesia sketching to the third position with a 6.17 percent share in this category, thereby displaying a low import dependence. The profile highlights that a majority of the ASEAN members constitute a very low percent share. Countries such as Brunei, Cambodia, Malaysia and Lao PDR almost display a same average percent share of 8.78.

Rising independence product lines displays a revealed import dependency (RID) value to be greater than unity, but witnessed a declining share during 2001-2015. Table 10.6 clearly explains that Lao PDR has the highest percent share of 9.15 followed by Brunei and Cambodia with a similar 8.60 percent share and Malaysia standing with a 7.18 percent share, depicting a greater comparative advantage with low import dependence. Major ASEAN members such as Singapore and

Philippines exhibit a low share percentage of 2.31 and 2.71 respectively under rising independence product category, thereby showing a high degree of import dependence. The RID profile spotlights that there exists a lower percentage share in rising independence products for India, which is considered to be an alarming situation for 'miscellaneous products' (HS 94-96) and 'wood and wood products' (HS 44-46).

Table 10.6: RID Profile for Mineral Fuel Manufactures (2001-2015)

Country	RD	ET (I)	ET (II)	LT (I)	LT (II)	RI	Total
Brunei	69 (45.6)	12 (7.9)	19 (12.5)	7 (4.6)	31 (20.5)	13 (8.6)	151 (8.1)
Cambodia	20 (13.1)	13 (8.5)	59 (38.8)	5 (3.2)	42 (27.6)	13 (8.6)	152 (8.1)
India	9 (5.1)	7 (3.9)	85 (48.2)	11 (6.2)	55 (31.2)	9 (5.1)	176 (9.4)
Indonesia	37 (20.7)	11 (6.1)	50 (28.0)	16 (8.9)	55 (30.8)	9 (5.0)	178 (9.5)
Lao	19 (12.4)	15 (9.8)	60 (39.2)	6 (3.9)	39 (25.4)	14 (9.1)	153 (8.2)
Malaysia	32 (17.6)	16 (8.8)	73 (40.3)	6 (3.3)	41 (22.6)	13 (7.1)	181 (9.7)
Myanmar	50 (29.9)	18 (10.7)	99 (59.2)	-	-	-	167 (8.9)
Philippines	48 (26.0)	22 (11.9)	61 (33.1)	4 (2.1)	44 (23.9)	5 (2.7)	184 (9.8)
Singapore	32 (18.4)	25 (14.4)	34 (19.6)	13 (7.5)	65 (37.5)	4 (2.3)	173 (9.2)
Thailand	36 (19.5)	29 (15.7)	52 (28.2)	16 (8.6)	41 (22.2)	10 (5.4)	184 (9.8)
Vietnam	30 (18.4)	9 (5.5)	50 (30.6)	7 (4.2)	56 (34.3)	11 (6.7)	163 (8.7)

Note: Numbers in parenthesis are percentage shares in the respective product line.

Notes: RD = Rising Dependence Products; RI = Rising Independence Products; ET (I) = Emerging Threatened Products Tier-I; ET (II) Emerging Threatened Products Tier-II; LT (I) = Less Threatened Products Tier-I and LT (II) = Less Threatened Products Tier-II.

Source: UNCOMTRADE; calculations by the researcher.

11

India-ASEAN Trade: Competitive Positioning of Imports at Industry Level

11.1 Non-fuel Primary Commodities

The total number of commodities under the non-fuel primary product line in India's import basket increased from 821 in 2010 to 845 in 2015. This marks a 24 percent change in less competitively positioned product line with a RID index greater than 1 and also a negative change of 2 percent in competitively positioned product line with a RID less than 1, thereby stating the emergence of import dependence of India for non-fuel primary commodities (Table 11.1).

On the contrary, ASEAN members such as Brunei, Malaysia, Lao, Philippines and Indonesia hold a comparative disadvantage with a heavy dependence on imports for non-fuel primary commodities with an exponential rise in percent share of less competitively positioned product line having a RID value greater than 1 with their respective values slated at 52, 38, 39, 36 and 29 percent in 2015 in comparison with 47, 30, 31, 27 and 27 percent in 2010. This also marks a decline in the competitively positioned product line having a RID less than 1 for 2015. Singapore and Vietnam hold comparative advantage in the non-fuel primary commodities with less of dependence on imports. Singapore reveals a high percent share of 80 in competitively positioned product line having a RID value less than 1 in 2015 with an increase in total number of products from 864 in 2010 to 1,013 in 2015. Similarly, Vietnam also reveals a comparative advantage with a 78 percent share in RID value less than 1 product line in 2015 and also a rise in the total number of products from 817 in 2010 to 994 in 2015.

Table 11.1: Profile for Non-Fuel Primary Manufactures (2010-2015)

Country	Product line with RID>1			Product line with RID<1		
	2010	2015	Percent Change	2010	2015	Percent Change
Brunei	286 (47)	320 (44)	12	326 (53)	393 (56)	21
Cambodia	77 (19)	94 (24)	22	318 (81)	347 (76)	9
India	152 (19)	188 (23)	24	669 (81)	657 (77)	-2
Indonesia	236 (27)	252 (29)	7	631 (73)	539 (71)	-15
Lao	136 (31)	173 (39)	27	307 (69)	381 (61)	24
Malaysia	272 (30)	345 (38)	27	646 (70)	816 (62)	26
Myanmar	79 (25)	105 (33)	33	243 (75)	480 (67)	98
Philippines	228 (27)	296 (36)	30	604 (73)	552 (64)	-9
Singapore	130 (15)	173 (20)	33	734 (85)	840 (80)	14
Thailand	203 (23)	295 (33)	45	692 (77)	761 (67)	10
Vietnam	233 (29)	182 (22)	-22	584 (71)	812 (78)	39

contd...

Country	Total No. of Product Lines		
	2010	2015	Percent Change
Brunei	612	713	14
Cambodia	395	441	10
India	821	845	3
Indonesia	867	791	-10
Lao	443	554	20
Malaysia	918	1161	21
Myanmar	322	585	45
Philippines	832	848	2
Singapore	864	1013	15
Thailand	895	1056	15
Vietnam	817	994	18

Note: Numbers in parenthesis are percentage shares in the respective product line.
Source: UNCOMTRADE; calculations by the researcher.

11.2 Resource Intensive Manufactures

The overall position of India in resource intensive manufactures exhibits an exponential increase in the import dependence with total number of products rising from 116 in 2010 to 908 in 2015 marking a 51 percent share in less competitive positioned product line having a RID index value to be greater than 1 in 2015.

On the contrary, ASEAN members depict a mixed trend

towards resource intensive manufactures. Singapore and Malaysia are the top most economies with least import dependence in spite of a mere increase of one percent in less competitively positioned product line with a RID value greater than 1. Table 11.2 reveals that Singapore holds a competitive advantage with a high percentage share of 87 percent in 2015 for product line having a RID index value to be less than 1, in comparison to only 13 percent in RID value greater than 1 in 2015. Similarly, Malaysia also exhibits a comparative advantage. Out of a total number of 1,122 products in 2015, 893 (which constitutes an 80 percent share), lies under the competitively positioned product line with a RID value less than unity.

Countries such as Indonesia, Myanmar and Philippines demonstrate a rise in import dependence for resource intensive manufactures. From Table 11.2, it could be clearly deduced that Indonesia, Myanmar and Philippines show an exponential increase in percent share in import dependence product line having a RID value to be greater than 1 with their respective values standing at 33, 37 and 34 percent in 2015, in comparison with a 29, 36 and 24 percent share in 2010. Lastly, the table also reveals a decline in percentage share for low import dependence product line possessing a RID value less than 1 with respective values positioned at 67, 63 and 66 percent in 2015, in comparison with 71, 64 and 76 percent in 2010.

Lastly, countries such as Laos and Vietnam, display a decline in import dependency for resource intensive manufactures with a negative trend in percentage change of -16 and -1 in more import dependence product line having a RID value greater than 1, followed by an increase in percent share from 62 in 2010 to 73 in 2015 for Indonesia and 63 percent in 2010 to 66 percent in 2015 for Vietnam in less import dependence product line possessing RID of less than one. It can easily be inferred from this analysis that India is heavily import dependent and thereby losing its competitive positioning in resource intensive manufactures. Hence, India should formulate trade policies to achieve a sustainable competitiveness and less import dependency in this particular industry level.

Table 11.2: Profile for Resource Intensive Manufactures (2010-2015)

Country	Product line with RID>1			Product line with RID<1		
	2010	2015	Percent Change	2010	2015	Percent Change
Brunei	281 (39)	290 (38)	3	448 (61)	480 (62)	7
Cambodia	161 (33)	192 (30)	19	323 (67)	443 (70)	37
India	116 (45)	908 (51)	683	141 (55)	871 (49)	518
Indonesia	297 (29)	352 (33)	19	729 (71)	713 (67)	-2
Lao	240 (38)	201 (27)	-16	387 (62)	534 (73)	38
Malaysia	168 (17)	229 (20)	36	840 (83)	893 (80)	6
Myanmar	169 (36)	333 (37)	97	306 (64)	568 (63)	86
Philippines	251 (24)	378 (34)	51	795 (76)	745 (66)	-6
Singapore	122 (12)	141 (13)	16	879 (88)	932 (87)	6
Thailand	220 (21)	248 (22)	13	827 (79)	865 (78)	5
Vietnam	370 (37)	368 (34)	-1	626 (63)	709 (66)	13

contd...

Country	Total No. of Product Lines		
	2010	2015	Percent Change
Brunei	729	770	6
Cambodia	484	635	31
India	257	1779	592
Indonesia	1026	1065	4
Lao	627	735	17
Malaysia	1008	1122	11
Myanmar	475	901	90
Philippines	1046	1123	7
Singapore	1001	1073	7
Thailand	1047	1113	6
Vietnam	996	1077	8

Note: Numbers in parenthesis are percentage shares in the respective product line.

Source: UNCOMTRADE; calculations by the researcher.

11.3 Low Skill and Technology Intensive Manufactures

The industry level of low skill and technology intensive manufactures has been illustrated in Table 11.3. This industry level investigates the inclusive vista of India with respect to other ASEAN members. A minor shift towards low import dependence has been observed from India's perspective. The table depicts a percentage share of 76 for 2015 in less import dependent positioned product line with a RID value to be less than 1 and on the contrary, a negative decline of -5 percent reveals India's less import dependence for low skill and technology intensive manufactures.

Table 11.3: Profile for Low Skill and Technology Intensive Manufactures

(2010-2015)

Country	Product line with RID>1			Product line with RID<1		
	2010	2015	Percent Change	2010	2015	Percent Change
Brunei	181 (48)	177 (46)	-2	200 (52)	202 (54)	1
Cambodia	71 (23)	101 (32)	42	244 (77)	260 (68)	7
India	122 (25)	116 (24)	-5	358 (75)	345 (76)	-4
Indonesia	216 (45)	227 (47)	5	269 (55)	253 (53)	-6
Lao	150 (39)	140 (37)	-7	233 (61)	276 (63)	18
Malaysia	151 (31)	152 (31)	1	332 (69)	352 (69)	6
Myanmar	146 (43)	148 (44)	1	191 (57)	290 (66)	52
Philippines	79 (17)	148 (31)	87	397 (83)	348 (69)	-12
Singapore	98 (21)	102 (22)	4	362 (79)	416 (78)	15
Thailand	167 (35)	206 (43)	23	313 (65)	310 (57)	-1
Vietnam	204 (43)	165 (35)	-19	270 (57)	327 (65)	21

contd...

Country	Total No. of Product Lines		
	2010	2015	Percent Change
Brunei	381	379	-1
Cambodia	315	361	15
India	480	461	4
Indonesia	485	480	-1
Lao	383	416	9
Malaysia	483	504	4
Myanmar	337	438	30
Philippines	476	496	4
Singapore	460	518	13
Thailand	480	516	8
Vietnam	474	492	4

Note: Numbers in parenthesis are percentage shares in the respective product line.
Source: UNCOMTRADE; calculations by the researcher.

ASEAN members such as Philippines, Thailand and Indonesia hold comparative disadvantage in low skill and technology intensive manufactures with a high import dependency. Philippines reveal an increase in total number of products from 79 in 2010 to 148 in 2015, marking a 87 percent change in less competitively positioned product line with a RID index to be greater than unity.

Similarly, Thailand and Indonesia also demonstrate an increase in percentage share with their respective values pegged at 43 and 47 percent in 2015 in comparison with 35 and 45 percent in 2010 for product line having a RID greater than 1 and simultaneously showing a decrease in percentage share for product line having RID less than unity from 55 and 65 percent in 2010 to 53 and 60 percent in 2015.

Lastly, ASEAN members such as Brunei, Lao and Vietnam also hold comparative advantage in low skill and technology intensive manufactures with a low import dependency. The percentage share of Brunei, Lao and Vietnam shows a declining trend in import dependency product line having a RID value greater than 1 with their respective percent share at 46, 37 and 35 in 2015, in comparison with 48, 39 and 43 percent in 2010. Moreover, the table also showcases an increasing trend in low import dependency product line with a RID of less than 1 for 2015 with a high percent share of 54, 66, and 65 percent respectively as illustrated in Table 11.3.

However, Malaysia experiences no change in competitive positioning in low skill and technology intensive manufactures. Percentage share for both competitively positioned product line remained constant for 2010 and 2015.

11.4 Medium Skill and Technology Intensive Manufactures

Under the medium skill and technology intensive manufactures industry level, India exhibits its comparative advantage with an increasing percentage share from 69 percent in 2010 to 74 percent in 2015 for low import dependency product line having a RID value to be less than unity accompanied by a decline in the total products from 228 in 2010 to 213 in 2015, revealing a -7 percent change in heavily import dependent product line having a RID value to be greater than 1.

On the other hand, ASEAN member countries such as Cambodia, Lao and Vietnam reveal a rise in comparative advantage with low import dependence for medium skill and technology intensive manufactures. Cambodia displays an increase in total number of products from 445 in 2010 to 473 in 2015 with a 6 percent change followed by a -7 percent change in less competitively positioned product line having RID value greater than 1. Similarly, Lao and Vietnam also reveal an increase in percent share for low import dependent product line having RID less than 1 with their respective percentage share at 67 and 55 percent for 2015 in comparison with a percentage share of 63 and 55 percent in 2010, thereby positioning them under the less import dependent countries.

The rest of the ASEAN members exhibit a decline in comparative advantage with a rising import dependency for medium skill and technology intensive manufactures. Countries such as Singapore, Thailand, Philippines, Malaysia and Indonesia reveal a high percentage share in import dependent product line having a RID index value to be greater than unity with their respective percentage share of 25, 44, 39, 40 and 57 percent for 2015 in comparison with 24, 41, 23, 41 and 54 percent share for 2010, hence depicting a rising dependence on imports for medium skill and technology intensive manufactures (Table 11.4).

11.5. High Skill and Technology Intensive Manufactures

Table 11.5 gives description of the high skill and technology intensive manufactures revealing that India has a rising import dependency in the particular industry level with an increase in import dependence from 345 products in 2010 to 383 products in 2015, an 11 percent change in import dependence product line having a RID value to be greater than 1 and also a declining percent share from 66 percent in 2010 to 61 percent in 2015 under the low import dependence product line having a RID value less than unity.

Table 11.4: Profile for Medium Skill and Technology Intensive Manufactures

(2010-2015)

Country	Product line with RID>1			Product line with RID<1		
	2010	2015	Percent Change	2010	2015	Percent Change
Brunei	189 (29)	223 (35)	18	453 (71)	421 (65)	-7
Cambodia	150 (25)	106 (18)	-29	445 (75)	473 (82)	6
India	228 (31)	213 (26)	-7	519 (69)	598 (74)	15
Indonesia	394 (53)	434 (57)	10	355 (47)	327 (43)	-8
Lao	233 (37)	219 (33)	-6	401 (63)	453 (67)	13
Malaysia	289 (41)	310 (40)	7	416 (59)	472 (60)	13
Myanmar	208 (34)	291 (39)	40	403 (66)	446 (61)	11
Philippines	179 (23)	307 (39)	72	592 (77)	475 (61)	-20
Singapore	180 (24)	199 (25)	11	566 (76)	588 (75)	4
Thailand	310 (41)	351 (44)	13	441 (59)	451 (56)	2
Vietnam	406 (54)	356 (45)	-12	342 (46)	427 (55)	25

contd...

Country	Total No. of Product Lines		
	2010	2015	Percent Change
Brunei	642	644	1
Cambodia	595	579	-3
India	747	811	9
Indonesia	749	761	2
Lao	634	672	6
Malaysia	705	782	11
Myanmar	611	737	21
Philippines	771	782	1
Singapore	746	787	5
Thailand	751	802	7
Vietnam	748	783	5

Note: Numbers in parenthesis are percentage shares in the respective product line.

Source: UNCOMTRADE; calculations by the researcher.

Major ASEAN members such as Indonesia, Malaysia, Philippines and Thailand also demonstrate an increasing competitive disadvantage with large import dependence for high skill and technology intensive manufactures. Table 6.23 illustrates an increase in the percentage share for import dependence product line possessing a RID greater than 1 for Indonesia, Malaysia, Philippines and Thailand with their respective percentage values pegged at 47, 40, 39 and 41 percent for 2015 in comparison to 43, 39, 35 and 39 percent for 2010, thereby, reflecting a comparative disadvantage in high skill and technology intensive manufactures.

Table 11.5: Profile for High Skill and Technology Intensive Manufactures

(2010-2015)

Country	Product line with RID>1			Product line with RID<1		
	2010	2015	Percent Change	2010	2015	Percent Change
Brunei	217 (33)	223 (32)	3	450 (67)	480 (68)	7
Cambodia	96 (18)	109 (17)	14	428 (82)	536 (83)	25
India	345 (34)	383 (39)	11	664 (66)	589 (61)	-11
Indonesia	438 (43)	473 (47)	8	575 (57)	541 (53)	-6
Lao	116 (21)	121 (19)	4	433 (79)	519 (81)	20
Malaysia	395 (39)	436 (40)	10	617 (61)	651 (60)	6
Myanmar	158 (27)	195 (24)	23	428 (73)	621 (76)	45
Philippines	366 (35)	430 (39)	17	689 (65)	667 (61)	-3
Singapore	262 (27)	283 (27)	8	726 (73)	757 (73)	4
Thailand	392 (39)	426 (41)	9	613 (61)	623 (59)	2
Vietnam	369 (38)	321 (32)	-13	610 (62)	688 (68)	13

contd...

Country	Total No. of Product line		
	2010	2015	Percent Change
Brunei	667	703	5
Cambodia	524	645	23
India	1009	972	-4
Indonesia	1013	1014	0
Lao	549	640	17
Malaysia	1012	1087	7
Myanmar	586	816	39
Philippines	1055	1097	4
Singapore	988	1040	5
Thailand	1005	1049	4
Vietnam	979	1009	3

Note: Numbers in parenthesis are percentage shares in the respective product line.

Source: UNCOMTRADE; calculations by the researcher.

Lastly, ASEAN members such as Brunei, Cambodia, Lao, Myanmar and Vietnam reveal a rising comparative advantage with low import dependence for high skill and technology intensive manufactures. Table 11.5 illustrates an increase in percentage share for low import dependence product line with RID value less than unity for Brunei, Cambodia, Lao, Myanmar and Vietnam with their respective percentage values at 68, 83, 81, 76 and 68 percent for 2015 in comparison to 67, 82, 79, 73 and 62 percent for 2010.

11.6 Mineral Fuel Manufactures

Total number of reported product line for India under the mineral fuel manufactures in 2010 were 148, out of which 129 products had a percent share of 87. By 2015, the percentage share decreased to 86 percent with 125 products. Also, the positive change of 5 percent in import dependence product line with a RID greater than 1 depicts a rise of comparative disadvantage or import dependence of India in mineral fuel manufactures.

On the contrary, ASEAN countries such as Brunei, Cambodia, Indonesia, Lao and Myanmar were swiftly emerging economies in mineral fuel manufactures, holding a higher comparative advantage of low import dependence in comparison with other ASEAN members. Lao exhibited a 41 percent change in low import dependency product line having RID value to be less than 1. It also exhibited an increase in percentage share in low import dependency product line having RID value less than 1 from 66 percent in 2010 to 78 percent in 2015. Similarly, Myanmar and Indonesia also demonstrated a rise in percentage share in low import dependence product line having RID less than 1 from 68 percent in 2010 to 71 percent in 2015 for Myanmar and 67 percent in 2010 to 71 percent share in 2015 for Indonesia, thereby reflecting low import dependence for these economies.

Major ASEAN countries such as Singapore, Philippines and Malaysia exhibit a slow rise in comparative disadvantage in mineral fuel manufactures with an increasing percentage share in import dependency product line having RID value greater than 1. Singapore, Philippines and Malaysia show a decline or fall in the percentage share for low import dependence product line having

RID value less than 1 from 85, 79 and 82 percent in 2010 to 80, 71 and 81 percent in 2015. These percentage figures exhibit a rise in import dependence of Singapore, Philippines and Malaysia in mineral fuel manufactures (Table 11.6).

Table 11.6: Table Profile for Mineral Fuel Intensive Manufactures

(2010-2015)

Country	Product line with RID>1			Product line with RID<1		
	2010	2015	Percent Change	2010	2015	Percent Change
Brunei	50 (40)	35 (27)	-30	75 (60)	94 (73)	25
Cambodia	29 (30)	27 (26)	-7	69 (70)	77 (74)	12
India	19 (13)	20 (14)	5	129 (87)	125 (86)	-3
Indonesia	49 (33)	42 (29)	-14	101 (67)	102 (71)	1
Lao	31 (34)	23 (22)	-26	59 (66)	83 (78)	41
Malaysia	26 (18)	29 (19)	12	121 (82)	126 (81)	4
Myanmar	27 (32)	39 (29)	44	58 (68)	94 (71)	62
Philippines	32 (21)	46 (29)	44	117 (79)	114 (71)	-3
Singapore	22 (15)	28 (20)	27	120 (85)	115 (80)	-4
Thailand	33 (22)	36 (23)	9	119 (78)	124 (78)	4
Vietnam	32 (25)	32 (23)	0	97 (77)	110 (77)	13

contd...

Country	Total No. of Product Lines		
	2010	2015	Percent Change
Brunei	125	129	3
Cambodia	98	104	6
India	148	145	-2
Indonesia	150	144	-4
Lao	90	106	18
Malaysia	147	155	5
Myanmar	85	133	56
Philippines	149	160	7
Singapore	142	143	1
Thailand	152	160	5
Vietnam	129	142	10

Note: Numbers in parenthesis are percentage shares in the respective product line.
Source: UNCOMTRADE; calculations by the researcher.

11.7 Conclusion

From the study, it could be inferred that amongst the six distinct industry levels, India demonstrates a rising trend in its import dependence under the non-fuel primary commodities in comparison with other ASEAN members. The rising percentage change under 'vegetable products' (HS 06-14) and 'mineral products' (HS 25-27) product line having RID value greater than 1 and the high combined percentage share under rising dependence and emerging threatened products reveals India's rising import dependence. ASEAN members such as Singapore and Vietnam have less of import dependence with a low percent share and a negative percent change in product line having RID value greater than 1. ASEAN nations such as Brunei, Cambodia, Indonesia and Lao also reveal their increasing dependence for imports.

Under the resource intensive manufactures category, India displays its rising import dependence for 'textile and textile products' (HS 50-63) product line lying under the respective industry level. With a tremendous increase in products from 116 in 2010 to 908 under the product line having RID value to be greater than 1 reveals an increasing import dependency of India. On the contrary, ASEAN members such as Vietnam, Thailand, Singapore, Malaysia etc. exhibit a low import dependency for resource intensive manufactures, thereby, revealing their competitive advantage over India. Under the low skill and technology intensive manufactures, India displays a declining trend in its import dependency for 'base metals and articles' (HS 72-83) with a negative percentage change in product line having RID greater than 1 and low percentage share for rising dependence products in comparison to other ASEAN members. India is still under the constant threat of competitive pressure from nations such as Vietnam, Myanmar, Malaysia and Lao PDR that are also registering a low percentage change for product line possessing RID value greater than unity.

India highlights a declining and diminishing import dependence under the medium skill and technology intensive manufactures industry level with a negative percentage change for 'machinery and mechanical appliances' (HS 84-85) product line having RID value less than 1 and also a low percent share for rising dependence product category. ASEAN members such as Vietnam, Lao PDR and Cambodia also demonstrate a shrinking import dependence.

For high skill and technology intensive manufactures category, India reveals import dependency for 'chemical products' (HS 28-38) with a high percentage share in rising dependence and emerging threatened products category followed by a higher percentage change in product line possessing RID value greater than 1. Vietnam, Thailand, Singapore and Lao PDR displays a less of import dependency with a low percent share in rising dependence product category and a low percentage change in product line having RID value greater than 1, in comparison to India, thereby demonstrating a rising threat to India's competitive advantage under the high skill and technology intensive manufactures.

Lastly, under the mineral fuel industry level, India reveals a rising import dependency with an increasing percent share under the emerging threatened products category and increasing percentage change for 'wood pulp products' (HS 47-49) and 'miscellaneous products' (HS 94-96) product line having RID value greater than one. On the contrary, ASEAN members such as Vietnam, Lao PDR, Indonesia, Cambodia and Brunei illustrate declining import dependence. Hence, to achieve a higher competitiveness, India should concentrate upon those industry levels where it poses a low import dependency and should also look up for import substitution policies for products which India imports more from other ASEAN members.

12

Conclusions and Policy Suggestions

This particular study reveals different aspects of the ASEAN-India Free Trade Agreement (AIFTA). In the current scenario, India-ASEAN relation seems to be important both politically and economically. ASEAN members have emerged as the main trading partners of India. The main aim of the study undertaken is to understand and unearth the dynamics of trade specialization and trade competitiveness of India-ASEAN in the context of free trade agreement (AIFTA) during the pre- and post-AIFTA scenario and hence the concluding essence is given below.

Ex-post result of ASEAN-India Free Trade Agreement (AIFTA) demonstrates that as far as trade is concerned, ASEAN has benefited more than India. The trends and pattern of ASEAN-India trade has been observed region-wise, commodity-wise and country-wise. An impressive rise in India's export to ASEAN region escalated from US$ 3.31 billion in 2001 to US$ 19.43 billion in 2008 and to US$ 37.88 billion during the year 2013, which is almost an enhancement of 11-12 times for the period 2001 to 2013. However, India registered a decline in its exports to US$ 26.42 billion for the year 2014-2015. Similarly, India's imports from ASEAN also demonstrated an exponential rising trend from US$ 4.3 billion in 2001 to US$ 29.6 billion in 2010 and to US$ 41.5 billion in 2015, which is an almost 9-10 times increase for the period 2001-2015. India's total trade with ASEAN members reveals an average annual growth of 19.2 percent from 2001-2015. From the region-wise study, it has been observed that India is facing a huge average trade deficit of US$ 5.62 billion per annum.

India's export growth in ASEAN region depicts a mixed trend. Initially, India's export growth to ASEAN region was more than the global export growth. But, India's export growth to ASEAN region witnessed a descending trend for two consecutive years which was -05.66 during the year 2014 and -16.74 in 2015. India's top 5 exporting commodities to ASEAN region includes mineral fuels, mineral oils and products (HS Code 27), meat and edible offal (HS Code 02), nuclear reactor, boilers, machinery and mechanical appliances (HS Code 84), organic chemicals (HS Code 29), and natural or cultured pearls, precious stones etc. (HS Code 71).

Correspondingly, India's import growth from ASEAN members registered a higher trend throughout the period of study with an average value of 18.86 percent from the year 2001 to 2015, in contrast to the average global import growth of 17.46 for the period 2001 to 2015. India's top 5 importing commodities from ASEAN included mineral fuels, mineral oils and products (HS Code 27), animal or vegetable fats and oil (HS Code 15), electrical machinery and equipments (HS Code 85), nuclear reactors, boilers, machinery and mechanical appliances (HS Code 84), and organic chemicals (HS Code 29).

ASEAN members including Singapore, Indonesia, Malaysia and Thailand are the prominent export destinations for India. India's exports to Singapore stood at an average of US$ 7.3 billion from 2001 to 2015 followed by Indonesia with US$ 2.9 billion and Malaysia ranking third in the list of largest exporting nation with an average of US$ 2.6 billion for the above mentioned period. ASEAN members such as Cambodia, Brunei and Lao PDR were the least favourable trade destinations for India in the ASEAN region. The study also highlights that India was also the net importer from same nations such as Indonesia, Singapore and Malaysia to whom it was a net exporter. India's net imports from Indonesia were the highest with an average volume of imports at US$ 7.58 billion from 2001 to 2015.

Thus, from the first objective of the study, it could be inferred that though there has been a tremendous increase in both the export and import structure of India, still ASEAN members are benefiting more from AIFTA. The mounting rise in the imports from ASEAN members and inflating average trade deficit of US$ 5.62 billion has been a matter of concern, thereby depicting that India's bilateral Free Trade Agreement (FTA) with ASEAN is statistically insignificant for India's import and export efficiency.

The direction of India-ASEAN trade has been rapidly shifting from less specialized economies towards more specialized economies. Under the non-fuel primary commodities, India reflects a mixed trend in trade specialization from 2001-02 to 2009-10, but after AIFTA, India experienced a decline in trade specialization in 2014-15 (LFI -0.52) for 'vegetable products' (HS 06-14), 'food stuff', (HS 16-24) and 'mineral products' (HS 25-27). ASEAN member Brunei has constantly experienced an exponential increase in its trade specialization.

On the other hand, ASEAN members such as Singapore and Thailand have experienced a constant decline in their trade specialization. India observed a varied trend in trade specialization for resource intensive manufactures for the time span 2001-2015. India experienced a decline in trade specialization from 2001-2010. But after AIFTA, India noticed a rise in trade specialization (LFI value 0. 64) for 2014-15 for 'textile and textile articles' (HS 50-63). ASEAN members Vietnam and Myanmar also experienced an exponential rise in their trade specialization. On the contrary, economies such as Indonesia and Malaysia lost their trade specialization constantly from 2001 to 2015.

Under the low skill and technology intensive manufactures, India observed a positive and a higher degree of trade specialization for 'base metals and articles' (HS 72-83) after AIFTA. With the passage of time, most of the ASEAN members such as Cambodia, Singapore, Thailand, Vietnam, Philippines and Lao PDR experienced a low improvement in trade specialization in comparison to India under the low skill and technology intensive manufactures.

Countries such as Brunei and Myanmar faced deterioration

in their trade specialization. For medium skill and technology intensive manufactures, India noticed a tremendous improvement in its trade specialization from low specialized nation to a positively high trade specialized nation for 'machinery and mechanical appliances' (HS 84-85) with LFI of 0.12 in 2014-15. On the other hand, ASEAN members such as Singapore, Thailand, Malaysia and Cambodia also demonstrated an improvement in trade specialization from 2001 to 2015. Countries such as Brunei, Lao PDR and Myanmar revealed a decline in trade specialization under a particular industry level.

Under the high skill and technology intensive manufactures, ASEAN members like Singapore, Thailand, Philippines and Malaysia were more specialized than India with positive LFI values. On the contrary, India also gained momentum under the particular industry level 'chemical products' (HS 28-38) product line with Lafay index value varying from -0.27 in 2001-02 to -0.18 in 2014-15.

Lastly, Indonesia and Brunei displayed a low level of trade specialization. India demonstrated a positive and high degree of trade specialization under mineral fuel industry level for 'miscellaneous products' (HS 94-96) and 'wood pulp' (HS 47-49) with respective LFI values of 0.23 in 2014-15. ASEAN members Singapore and Indonesia registered a higher degree of trade specialization and competitiveness under the mineral fuel industry level in comparison to India. Nations such as Brunei, Lao PDR, Malaysia and Thailand displayed deterioration of trade specialization with rising negative LFI values in 2014-15.

Hence, from the second objective of the study, it could be summarized that though India is swiftly moving towards achieving a higher degree of trade specialization, still it faces tough competition from the dynamic and vibrant ASEAN members such as Singapore, Malaysia, Philippines, Thailand and Vietnam. In a majority of industrial levels, after the AIFTA came into action, India experienced an improvement in its trade specialization irrespective of non-fuel primary commodities where India observed deterioration in its trade specialization. Therefore, India has to work upon a lot of spheres to attain a high trade specialization with respect to ASEAN members.

Ultimately, for determining trade competitiveness between India and ASEAN members, the revealed comparative advantage (RCA) and revealed import dependency (RID) method was taken into consideration. The analysis of the study leads to interesting observations. Amongst the six different industry levels as proposed by Basu and Das (2011), under non-fuel primary manufactures, percentage change of export competitiveness for India using the RCA approach was low in comparison with percentage change of import dependency using the RID approach, thereby exhibiting a decline and deterioration in India's trade competitiveness for non-fuel primary commodities such as 'vegetable products' (HS 06-14), 'food stuff' (HS 16-24) and 'mineral products' (HS 25-27) with respect to ASEAN members.

Under the low skill and technology intensive manufactures, India displayed a rising trend in its trade competitiveness for 'base metals and articles' (HS 72-83) with a high percentage change in exports under the competitive positioning profile using RCA and on the contrary, India observed a negative percentage change for import dependency under the RID competitive positioning profile. However, India is still experiencing competitive pressure from major ASEAN members such as Lao PDR, Malaysia, Philippines, Thailand and Vietnam. All these ASEAN members are registering a tremendously high percentage share under the competitive positioning of exports, revealing a threat to the competitive position of India.

India, demonstrated an improvement in its trade competitiveness for medium skill and technology intensive manufactures such as 'machinery and mechanical appliances' (HS 84-85). Industry levels display an escalating percentage rise in export competitiveness positioning using RCA approach in comparison with low import dependency positioning using the RID tool. On the contrary, India is constantly under the rising threat of increasing trade competitiveness of ASEAN members such as Malaysia, Philippines, Vietnam, Singapore and Thailand for medium skill and technology intensive manufactures, thereby revealing India's ascending competitive stress.

India posed a gaining momentum in its trade competitiveness for mineral fuel manufactures under the product line 'wood pulp products' (HS 47-49) and 'miscellaneous products' (HS 94-96). Percentage change under export competitive positioning is high in comparison to percent change under the import dependency position. Nations such as Thailand, Philippines and Vietnam exhibited a large percentage share for competitively positioned products under the RCA profile for mineral fuels thereby depicting a competitive advantage of these nations over India.

Somewhat different phenomenon happened under the resource intensive industry level with India portraying a decline and deterioration in its trade competitiveness for 'textile and textile articles' (HS 50-63). A high percentage share and change was observed under the import dependency positioning and a decline in percentage change and share for competitive positioning of export using the RCA approach. India has lost its competitive advantage over ASEAN members such as Malaysia, Philippines and Vietnam. Lastly, countries such as Myanmar and Singapore are the emerging threats for India under the resource intensive manufactures with a tremendously high percentage share under the emerging products category (Tier-I and Tier-II).

Lastly, under the high skill and technology intensive manufactures such as 'chemical products' (HS 28-38) and 'measuring and musical instruments' (HS 90-92), India is gaining its trade competitiveness with a higher percent change under the export competitive positioning using the RCA tool and on the contrary, a rise in import dependency under competitive positioning for India is low under a particular industry level. ASEAN nations such as Singapore, Philippines, Malaysia, Thailand and Vietnam possess better competitive positioning than India for high skill and technology intensive manufactures.

Therefore, from the third objective of the study, it could be inferred that to endure trade competitiveness, India should focus on those industry levels that are reflecting a comparative advantage and should also take measures in those industry levels where ASEAN members are possessing a higher percentage share for competitively positioned and emerging products. Thus, to gain competitiveness in this ever changing globalization, India should work more rigorously both at the micro and macro level.

Following are the policy suggestions arrived at by studying ASEAN-India relations in context of Free Trade Agreement:

- India needs to be more cautious before deciding to further liberalize the current AIFTA; which means including more products in the normal track list.
- More vigorous attempts need to be put in by India in strengthening its domestic industries and economic institutions, so that they are better equipped to overcome the future challenges of liberalization.
- India should confront issues such as skill level, nature of product and technology in use, scale of production, quality sophistication, reliability etc. at the industry level, which can constrain its 'export creation'.
- Under the non-fuel primary manufactures, India should put more efforts in reviving and strengthening the 'mineral products' (HS 25-27) and 'vegetable products' (HS 06-14) product line in which India is steadily losing its trade competitiveness and specialization in comparison with other ASEAN members.
- Rigorous efforts are need to be undertaken by India for lowering the import dependence from ASEAN members

for textile and textile articles (HS 50-63) product line falling under the resource intensive manufactures.

- Though India observes specialization and competitive advantage under both low and medium skill and technology intensive manufactures for base metals and articles (HS 72-83) and machinery and mechanical appliances (HS 84-85) product line, India should pursue a policy to overcome the stiff competitive pressure it faces from ASEAN members.
- India must concentrate on the commodity group that are of top-most priority and significance to ASEAN, so that Indian exports to the region may reach the targeted level.
- The extent to which India can thrive for higher value added export industries are those in which knowledge and technology intensive industries play a crucial role.
- Domestic capacity and quality of chemical products (HS 28-38) and measuring and musical instruments (HS 90-92) falling under the high skill and technology intensive category needs to be improvised using an effective regulatory framework, so that these products overcome the competitive pressure faced from other ASEAN members like Singapore, Vietnam, Thailand, Philippines and Malaysia.
- India needs to invest more in research and development (R&D) to have greater access to newer technologies and launch innovation techniques thereby achieving cost advantage and quality sophistication.

Annexures

Annexure 1

Non-fuel Primary Commodity Description: 2 Digit Harmonised System Code

Code	Product Label
1.	Live animals
2.	Meat and edible meat offal
3.	Fish, crustaceans, molluscs, aquatic invertebrates
4.	Dairy products, eggs, honey, edible animal products
5.	Products of animal origin
6.	Live trees, plants, bulbs, roots, cut flowers etc.
7.	Edible vegetables and certain roots and tubers
8.	Edible fruit, nuts, peel of citrus fruit, melons
9.	Coffee, tea, mate and spices
10.	Cereals
11.	Milling products, malt, starches, insulin, wheat gluten
12.	Oil seed, oleagic fruits, grain, seed, fruit, etc.
13.	Lac, gums, resins, vegetable saps and extracts
14.	Vegetable plaiting materials, vegetable products
15.	Animal, vegetable fats and oils, cleavage products
16.	Meat, fish and seafood food preparations
17.	Sugars and sugar confectionery
18.	Cocoa and cocoa preparations
19.	Cereal, flour, starch, milk preparations and products
20.	Vegetable, fruit, nut etc. food preparations
21.	Miscellaneous edible preparations
22.	Beverages, spirits and vinegar
24.	Tobacco and manufactured tobacco substitutes
25.	Salt, sulphur, earth, stone, plaster, lime and cement
26.	Ores, slag and ash
27.	Mineral fuels, oils, distillation products etc.

40.	Rubber and articles thereof
41.	Raw hides and skins (other than fur skins) and leather
43.	Fur skins and artificial fur, manufactures thereof
44.	Wood and articles of wood, wood charcoal
45.	Cork and articles of cork
47.	Pulp of wood, fibrous cellulosic material, waste etc.
51.	Wool, animal hair, horsehair yarn and fabric thereof
52.	Cotton
53.	Vegetable textile fibres nes, paper yarn, woven fabric
55.	Manmade staple fibres
71.	Pearls, precious stones, metals, coins etc.
74.	Copper and articles thereof
75.	Nickel and articles thereof
76.	Aluminium and articles thereof
78.	Lead and articles thereof
79.	Zinc and articles thereof
81.	Other base metals, cermets, articles thereof
82.	Tools, implements, cutlery etc. of base metal

Annexure 2

Resource Intensive Commodity Description: 2 Digit Harmonized System Code

Code	Product Label
40.	Rubber and articles thereof
41.	Raw hides and skins (other than fur skins) and leather
43.	Fur skins and artificial fur, manufactures thereof
44.	Wood and articles of wood, wood charcoal
45.	Cork and articles of cork
48.	Paper and paperboard, articles of pulp, paper and board
51.	Wool, animal hair, horsehair yarn and fabric thereof
52.	Cotton
53.	Vegetable textile fibres nes, paper yarn, woven fabric
54.	Manmade filaments
55.	Manmade staple fibres
56.	Wadding, felt, non-wovens, yarns, twine, cordage etc.
57.	Carpets and other textile floor coverings
58.	Special woven or tufted fabric, lace, tapestry etc.
59.	Impregnated, coated or laminated textile fabric
60.	Knitted or crocheted fabric
61.	Articles of apparel, accessories, knit or crochet
62.	Articles of apparel, accessories, not knit or crochet
63.	Other made textile articles, sets, worn clothing etc.
64.	Footwear, gaiters and the like, parts thereof
65.	Headgear and parts thereof
66.	Umbrellas, walking-sticks, seat-sticks, whips etc.

67.	Bird skin, feathers, artificial flowers, human hair
68.	Stone, plaster, cement, asbestos, mica etc. articles
69.	Ceramic products
70.	Glass and glassware
71.	Pearls, precious stones, metals, coins, etc.
94.	Furniture, lighting, signs, prefabricated buildings
95.	Toys, games, sports requisites

Annexure 3

Medium Skill and Technology Commodity: Description 2 digit Harmonized System code

Code	Product Label
39.	Plastics and articles thereof
40.	Rubber and articles thereof
84.	Machinery, nuclear reactors, boilers etc.
85.	Electrical, electronic equipment
87.	Vehicles other than railway, tramway
90.	Optical, photo, technical, medical etc. apparatus

Annexure 4

Low Skill and Technology Commodity: Description 2 Digit Harmonized System Code

Code	Product Label
72.	Iron and steel
73.	Articles of iron or steel
74.	Copper and articles thereof
75.	Nickel and articles thereof
76.	Aluminium and articles thereof
77.	Reserved for possible future use
78.	Lead and articles thereof
79.	Zinc and articles thereof
80.	Tin and articles thereof
81.	Other base metals, cermet's, articles thereof
82.	Tools, implements, cutlery etc. of base metal
83.	Miscellaneous articles of base metal
86.	Railway, tramway locomotives, rolling stock equipment
87.	Vehicles other than railway, tramway
89.	Ships, boats and other floating structures
94.	Furniture, lighting, signs, prefabricated buildings

Annexure 5

High Skill and Technology Commodity: Description 2 Digit Harmonized System Code

Code	Product Label
28.	Inorganic chemicals, precious metal compound, isotopes
29.	Organic chemicals
30.	Pharmaceutical products
31.	Fertilizers
32.	Tanning, dyeing extracts, tannins, derivs, pigments
33.	Essential oils, perfumes, cosmetics, toiletries
34.	Soaps, lubricants, waxes, candles, modelling pastes
35.	Albuminoids, modified starches, glues, enzymes
36.	Explosives, pyrotechnics, matches, pyrophorics.
37.	Photographic or cinematographic goods
38.	Miscellaneous chemical products
39.	Plastics and articles thereof
84.	Machinery, nuclear reactors, boilers etc.
85.	Electrical, electronic equipment
88.	Aircraft, spacecraft, and parts thereof
90.	Optical, photo, technical, medical etc. apparatus

Annexure 6

Mineral Fuel Commodity Description: 2 Digit Harmonized System Code

Code	Product Label
46.	Manufactures of plaiting material, basketwork
49.	Printed books, newspapers, pictures etc.
71.	Pearls, precious stones, metals, coins, etc.
85.	Electrical, electronic equipment
92.	Musical instruments, parts and accessories
93.	Arms and ammunition, parts and accessories thereof
96.	Miscellaneous manufactured articles
97.	Works of art, collectors pieces and antiques

References

References

Ahmed, S. (2010), "India-ASEAN Trade Agreement: A Sectoral Analysis", Working Paper No.1698849, available at: http://ssrn.com/abstract=1698849.

Alam, M.I. (2015), "Indo-ASEAN Trade Relations: An Analysis", *Journal of International Economics*, 6(1), 73.

Ambatkar, S. (2002), "An Evaluation of India-ASEAN Economic Cooperation since 1985", *Regional Studies-Islamabad,* 20(4), 72-97.

Arghyrou, G.M. and Bazina, E. (2003), "Competitiveness and the External Trade of Greece in the 1990s: A Cross-Sectoral Investigation", *Journal of Economic Integration*, 18(4), 763-793.

Balassa, B. (1961), "Towards a Theory of Economic Integration", *Kyklos*, 14(1), 1-17.

Banga, R. (2005), "Critical Issues in India's Service-led Growth", *Indian Council for Research on International Economic Relations*, 171(1), 1-18.

Banga, R. and Kumar, D. (2011), "India's Exports of Software Services: Role of External Demand and Productivity", *Science Technology and Society*, 16(3), 285-307.

Banik, N. and Centrale, M.E. (2014), "India-ASEAN Free Trade Agreement: The Untapped Potential", Working Paper No. 57954, available at: https://mpra.ub.uni muenchen.de/57954/1/MPRA_paper_57954.

Basu, S.R., and Das, M. (2011), "Export Structure and Economic Performance in Developing Countries: Evidence from Non-parametric Methodology", 8(1), 1-59.

Bhattacharyya, R. and Mandal, A. (2010), "Estimating the Impact of the Indo-ASEAN Free Trade Agreement on India's Balance of Trade", *Journal of Global Analysis*, 1(1), 9-25.

Brooks, D.H. and Menon, J. (2008), "Infrastructure and Trade in Asia" Cheltenham, U.K. and Northampton, Mass.: Elgar; Manila: Asian Development Bank, 2(13), 240.

Cairncross, A.K. (1960), "International Trade and Development", *Economica New Series*, 28(111), 235-251.

Chandran, S. and Sudarsan, P.K. (2012), "Revealed Comparative Advantage (RCA) and Trade Complementarity between India-

ASEAN Trade: A Study with Reference to Fisheries Sector", Working Paper No. 2054132.

Choudhary, S. (2013), "India and ASEAN Trade: An Overview", *International Journal of Social Science and Interdisciplinary Research*, 2(2), 143-156.

Civan, A. and Serin, V. (2008), "Revealed Comparative Advantage and Competitiveness: A Case Study for Turkey towards the EU", *Journal of Economic and Social Research*, 10(2), 25-41.

Cockerham, G.B. (2010), "Regional Integration in ASEAN: Institutional Design and the ASEAN Way", *East Asia*, 27(2), 165-185.

Diwan, R. and Chakraborty, C. (1993), "Is India's Economy Competitive?", *Economic and Political Weekly*, 28(45), 2478-2482.

Dutta, S. (1997), "India and ASEAN: A Framework for Comprehensive Engagement", *Strategic Analysis*, 20(3), 13-69.

Engelbrecht, H.J. (1998), "Business Sector R&D and Australia's Manufacturing Trade Structure", *Applied Economics*, 30(2), 177-189.

Fagerberg, J. (1988), "International Competitiveness", *The Economic Journal*, 98(391), 355-374.

Fagerberg, J. (2000), "Technological Progress, Structural Change and Productivity Growth: A Comparative Study", *Structural Change and Economic Dynamics*, 11(4), 393-411.

Fajnzylber, F. (1988), "International Competitiveness: Agreed Goal, Hard Task", *Cepal Review*, 36(1), 7-23.

Firend, R.A. (2016), "Asian Case Studies: Lessons from Malaysian Industries", *IJBMR Publisher*, 4-10.

Francis, S. (2011), "The ASEAN-India Free Trade Agreement: A Sectoral Impact Analysis of Increased Trade Integration in Goods", *Economic and Political Weekly*, 46(2), 46-55.

Gomes, J. (2002), "Competitiveness through Privatisation", *Economic and Political Weekly*, 37(19), 1789-1790.

Harilal, K.N. (2010), "ASEAN-India Free Trade Area: Noises of Dissent from Deep South", *Journal of International Economics*, 11(3), 21-32.

Haokip, T. (2011), "India's Look East Policy: Its Evolution and Approach", *South Asian Survey*, 18(2), 239-257.

Hausmann, R., Hwang, J. and Rodrik, D. (2007), "What You Export Matters", *Journal of Economic Growth*, 12(1), 1-25.

Index

Index